*Also by* WILLIAM K. EVERSON
The Western
The American Movie

# THE BAD GUYS

# THE

THE CITADEL PRESS

SECAUCUS, NEW JERSEY

# BAD GUYS

A Pictorial History
of the Movie Villain

by

WILLIAM K. EVERSON

Seventh paperbound printing, 1974
Copyright © 1964 by William K. Everson
All rights reserved
Published by Citadel Press
A division of Lyle Stuart, Inc.
120 Enterprise Ave., Secaucus, N. J. 07094
In Canada: George J. McLeod Limited
73 Bathurst St., Toronto, Ont.
Manufactured in the United States of America
Designed by William Meinhardt
ISBN 0-8065-0198-7

Dedicated to

## CHARLES KING

who never quite scaled the heights, but who was *the* badman to all of us who bounced up and down on our seats at Saturday matinees through the thirties and forties.

# ACKNOWLEDGMENTS

Especially grateful thanks are due to Gerald D. McDonald whose extensive still collection provided some of the rarest photographs in this volume. Further thanks are due to Carlos Clarens, Charles Turner, Herman G. Weinberg, Edward Connor, Alex Gordon, Dan Phillips, and John E. Allen for the loan of key stills from their collections.

# FOREWORD

The history of the "bad guys" is, in a sense, the history of the movies themselves. The bad guys commanded our attention from the very first—before there were heroes, before there were heroines, even before there were real plots—and they've never let it go. Vice has always been more fascinating than virtue, and because most of us never have the *serious* inclination—or perhaps the right opportunity—to explore it more thoroughly, we've settled happily for exploring it by proxy in novels and, in the 20th century, on the movie screen. Psychologists assure us that crime and violence on the screen is healthy, because it purges us of those repressed tendencies. Whether it does is something for the doctors to argue over, but the inescapable fact remains that crime on the screen is *fun*, for us, the audience. In a world increasingly rampant with restrictions and laws and codes, it's good to see authority being deflated, laws ignored, and stifling order turned into exhilarating chaos. And it's comforting, too to be reminded—as the last reels invariably do—that the law-breaker must pay the piper, and that despite excesses, most laws are quite endurable!.

The activities of the bad guys tell us far more about the changing mores and morals of our times than a similar study of the good guys could ever do. From time's beginning, the basic *virtues* have remained unchanged. But social, moral, and legal behavior is forever changing. Actions that might be unthinkable in one era, and would inevitably brand their perpetrator as a bad guy, might be perfectly acceptable a decade or two later. And it is strictly a one-way traffic. While certain virtues may come to be regarded as old-fashioned, or, in current vernacular, "square," they never quite regress into becoming antisocial. Conversely, more and more patterns of social behavior that were once considered totally unacceptable are being adopted, sometimes with modifications, often without, into our current way of life. The movies offer a staggering commentary on this ever-present change by their reflection of the times and tempos of the past sixty years.

If *The Bad Guys* helps to comment on this aspect of the movies, and to bring it into sharper focus, so much the better. But its principal object is not a sociological one, but is rather to offer a nostalgic and light-hearted, but withal respectful survey of one aspect of the movies—the wonderful heavies, brutes, monsters, mad doctors, train robbers, gangsters, and pirates—good badmen and *bad* badmen—who have made those movies so exciting, and such fun.

Obviously, there are going to be some omissions. It would have been possible to devote this book entirely to western heavies, devoting one chapter to cattle rustlers, and another to stagecoach robbers. And there are going to be overlaps. Basil Rathbone played pirates, wife-murderers, child-beaters, corrupt officials, Nazis, and madmen—all of them superbly. So did many other fine character actors. Some of them may turn up in these pages in several categories; others may be represented by the one standout role by which they are universally recognized. And what of the romantic stars who would doubtless be insulted to find themselves casually listed as bad guys? Do Ronald Colman, Herbert Marshall, Stewart Granger, John Wayne, and William Holden deserve to rub shoulders with Boris Karloff, Erich von Stroheim, and Noah Beery? Yet, recall that Robert Taylor, one of the most handsome romantic idols of the 1930's, later played such roles as a Communist spy, a western badman, a psychotic killer, a gangster, and a crooked cop, all within the space of a few years.

The answer is that crime in the movies, like crime in real life, is full of fringe cases. It's up to the judge whether they go to jail, or are set free. Personal favorites, "landmark" villains, and heavies who, by sheer consistency if not actual achievement demand recognition, present no problems. They are here. And if your particular favorite was a fringe "suspect" who got away this time, bear with us. Doubtless a later volume will catch him, and put him where he belongs.

# CONTENTS

# THE BAD GUYS

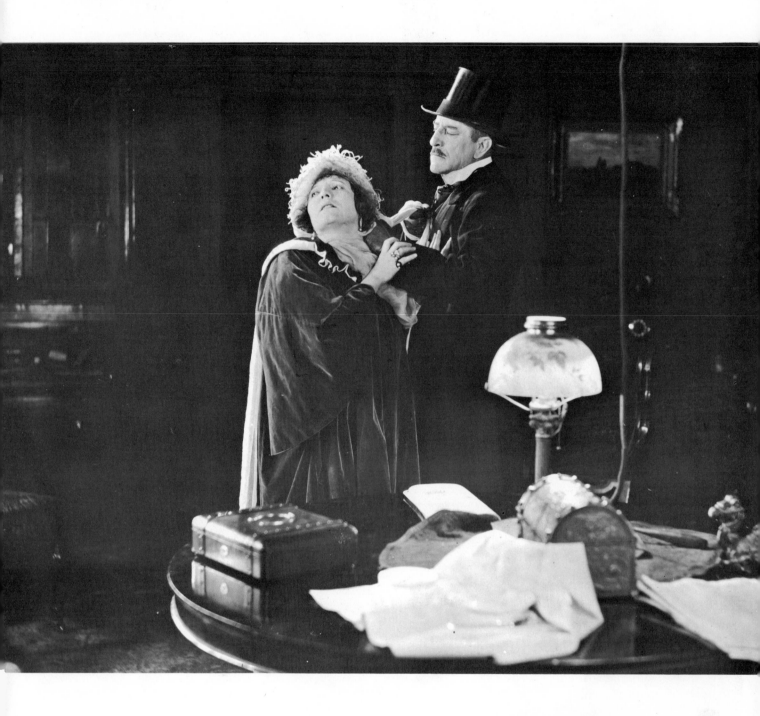

# THE EARLY
## VILLAINS

Unknown and unbilled extras play western bandits in 1903's *The Great Train Robbery*.

The movies had bad guys long before they had good guys—or, for that matter, good gals either. Edison's 1903 landmark, *The Great Train Robbery*, the film that really introduced crime to the movies and proved that there at least, it could pay, had neither hero nor heroine. But it did have a whole gang of outlaws, who, in the course of some nine minutes of film, committed at least two definite murders, some other *probable* ones in the heat of battle, terrorized a train-load of passengers, pulled off the robbery of the title, and shot it out with the sheriff's posse.

From almost the very beginning, the pioneer movie-makers seemed to sense that the lawless were more exciting than the law-abiding. To be sure, Edwin S. Porter made his *Life of an American Policeman* and *Life of an American Fireman*, but such tributes to the majesty of law-abiding institutions were rare. Far more common were such titles as *A Desperate Encounter between Burglars and Police*, *The Ruffian's Reward*, and *The Fire Bug*. Perhaps because it was already deemed good showmanship, crime never paid in these early vignettes, which seldom ran more than five minutes. It's more likely, however, that the movies, considered far from respectable then, were in fact trying to prove just how respectable they were via these filmed moral lessons that proved how dangerous and unprofitable crime was. No really clearly defined "bad guys" came out of these 1900 to 1906 films, however. They were just thugs, and usually showed it by being unshaven, using heavy black eye-make-up, and wearing what the movies considered to be standard burglar or hoodlum outfits. Since there were no stars as yet, there was no way of telling if one studio's bad guy had more talent than another's.

Two members of D. W. Griffith's stock company, Alfred Paget (in rear) and Charles H. Mailes, make their escape on a handcar, having stolen the payroll and abducted the telegraphist (Dorothy Bernard). A scene from Griffith's *A Girl and Her Trust* (1912).

Indeed, since film grammar still awaited its evolution under the guidance of master-director D. W. Griffith, there were so few close-ups utilized that it was often impossible to get a good look at the bad guys anyway.

But, from 1908 on, the movies began to grow up. They had advanced now from vignettes and single situations to complete stories, told surprisingly well in the ten to fifteen minute span of a single reel. The heroes of these little tales were often quite colorless, and it was the villains were provided the bulk of the plot motivation. Most of Griffith's excellent little suspense thrillers such as *The Lonely Villa* and *A Girl and Her Trust* created tension by having the heroine *constantly* menaced by the villains, with only occasional cutaways to the hero putting rescue plans into operation. The motive was usually quite simple: robbery. In fact, *all* villainy was simple in those early years. Influenced to a large degree by the melodramatic Victorian novels of the previous decade, the movies were full of such situations as a girl taking on a man's job (for example, a telegraph operator) and proving herself able to handle all emergencies as well as a man—including the outwitting of robbers. Of course, the poor heroine, saddled with both an ailing mother *and* a lecherous landlord, came in for her fair share of attention too. But, old-fashioned as some of these films may sound in one-line synopsis form, many of them had a great deal of power, and, considering that the movies were still so young, were skilfully done. Nor were the movies reluctant to tackle big or seemingly controversial themes either: villains in some of Griffith's early one-reelers ranged from a ruthless manufacturer of soft drinks (Dopocoke) who spiked

Paget again, at right, as the head of a smuggling gang in another exciting Griffith melodrama of 1912, *The Lesser Evil*. Blanche Sweet is his captive.

Paul Panzer, the gesticulating villain of the first Pearl White serial, *The Perils of Pauline*.

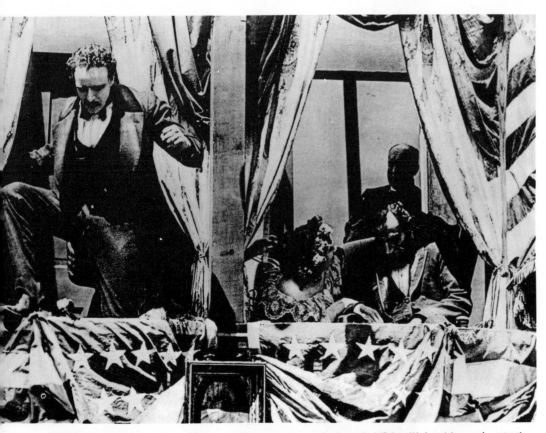

Raoul Walsh, later to become a top director, was another Griffith villain. Above, in 1915's *The Birth of a Nation*, he played John Wilkes Booth, and is leaping to the stage of Ford's Theatre following his assassination of President Lincoln (Joseph Henaberry, likewise soon to become a director).

The best early villains, it seems, all worked for D. W. Griffith. Walter Long is impressed with Lillian Gish in *Sold for Marriage* (1916).

his product with cocaine, and turned his son and fiancée into drug addicts, to the callous Count Dmitri of Tolstoy's *Resurrection* who seduced a peasant girl and caused her to work in a brothel when her baby died.

In those years, the villains were beginning to divide themselves, slowly, into types. Already, by 1910, there were sophisticated villains, hoodlums, brutes, and other clearly defined types. But there were not as yet equally clearly defined faces to go along with these types. Most of the companies in these pre-star-system days handled their players in stock-company fashion. Charles West played the dope addict villain in *For His Son*, but he also played the sensitive hero in other movies. Charles Mailes was a lecherous seducer in *Two*

*Paths*—so lecherous that the film was at pains to suggest that he was actually Satan himself—but in another film he was a dignified father. Most players still weren't even identified by name, so audiences had no way of picking their favorite villains except by describing his visual characteristics.

But, by 1914, the movies had changed quite a bit. They were on their way to becoming an art. They were already big business. Features of five reels were commonplace now, and, sparked by names like Mary Pickford, Charlie Chaplin, Helen Gardner, and Maurice Costello, the star system had arrived—to skyrocket salaries, production costs—and box office receipts. And once a player became a star, there was no stock-company fluctuating between good guys and

6

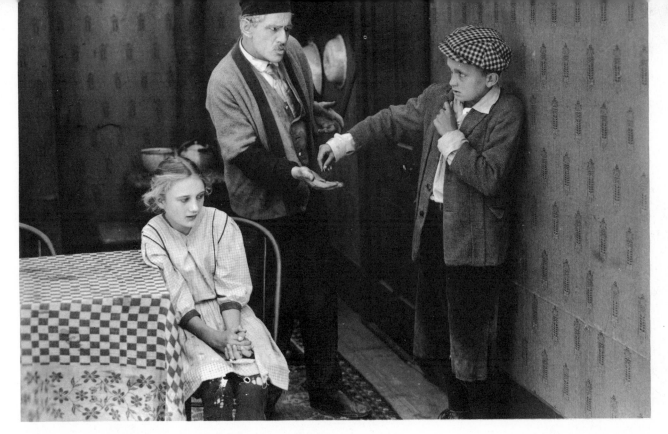

A tyrannical stepfather was an ever-reliable heavy in the early days. Here Edward Warren plays the role, with Violet Wilkey and Harold Goodwin (to grow up into a movie villain himself) as his victims in the 1916 *The Little Orphans*.

Costumes clearly establish social status here: hat and pin-stripes leave no doubt that William Lowery is the head of the gang. His minions rate no better than dark suits and caps. The villains from a 1916 Douglas Fairbanks film, *Reggie Mixes In*.

Warner Oland starts his career of Oriental skulduggery as the heavy in Pearl White's 1917 serial, *The Fatal Ring*.

bad guys. He had to be somebody the audience could root for all the time. Out of this, came an equally important need—somebody the audience could hiss all the time. Thus, the first real full-fledged, full-time villains came to the movies. Sheldon Lewis . . . Walter Long . . . Montague Love . . . Noah Beery . . . and perhaps most important of all the "pioneer" villains, Paul Panzer. It was Panzer who menaced Pearl White in the 1914 serial *The Perils of Pauline*, and he conveniently encompassed several different brands of villainy. First, he was ruthless, with no regard at all for human life. Second, he was cunning and crafty. Playing Pearl's guardian, he tried to kill her off from the first chapter to the last, and never once did Pearl tumble to the double-game he was playing. He betrayed her at every turn, set her out to sea in a leaky boat, sprinkled barbed metal on the road hoping to wreck her racing car, and tried poison, time bombs, snakes, and every other conceivable mode of execution in his efforts to dispatch her. But, even in the final episode, when his own treachery had rebounded on himself and he had gone to a watery grave, Pearl seemed naively unaware of his perfidy. On the other hand, she didn't seem unduly distressed by her guardian's sudden demise, either.

Panzer, dressed to the hilt and usually sporting jack boots and a deer-stalker hat, gave his villainy a robust exuberance that seemed to have even greater gusto when compared with the rather underplayed heroics of Pearl White. He'd grimace, shake his fist, pantomime his newest scheme, and gloat gleefully in anticipation of its successful execution. It was a brand of villainy deriving from the stage, and the stage of a decade or two earlier at that. But, in *The Perils of Pauline*, it worked, and while one was never convinced of, or scared by, his villainy (the villain's name was Koerner, since obviously no American could be as double-dyed as he was!), one was certainly entertained by it. Panzer was in the movies until the 1950's. Somehow, he always seemed to be playing Koerner—and perhaps because of that never became a really important silent villain. Koerner was both his limitation—and his major charm. And too, Koerner was somewhat of a grand last stand for the Victorian villain. Obviously, from now on, the movies had to be subtler. And they were. But *The Perils of Pauline* and Paul Panzer provided a wonderful swan-song for the delightful "Curses! Foiled Again!" brand of villainy that was actually far less prevalent in the early movies than is generally supposed.

8

# THE VILLAIN'S
# VILLAIN

In almost all other categories in this book, the need for a certain order and discipline has meant the elimination of many villains who, delightful as they might be, just weren't heinous enough to come to the head of their particular class. But here there can be no quibbling; we must bow to the two undisputed masters: Noah Beery Sr., and Montague Love. Both were mustachioed blackguards of the old school, swaggering scoundrels who loved villainy for its own sake, and who had not a single redeeming feature—except possibly a sense of humor. They sensed the audience enjoyment to be gained from all-out villainy, and, for the most part, played their heavies tongue-in-cheek, although both were good enough (and dedicated enough) actors to turn the menace on seriously when the role so demanded. Both looked sufficiently jolly and cherubic to play Santa Claus, but it would have been a Santa Claus with a very un-Christmassy glint in his eyes. Sheer lust was their common denominator, and no amount of thievery and murder meant very much to them unless a chance to despoil a young maiden went along with it!

Noah Beery outfought by Douglas Fairbanks in *The Mark of Zorro* (1920).

British-born Montague Love got his first real taste of villainy at Fort Lee's old World Studios, where, in the pre-1920 years, he was the perennial villain in the vehicles of Alice Brady—vehicles that included such Ruritanian costume melodramas as *The Gilded Cage*. The fact that Miss Brady was rather a homely young lady put no damper on Love's efforts at seduction. But he really came into his own with the grand-scale adventure extravaganzas of the late 1920's. Since these were largely tongue-in-cheek in approach, his own larger-than-life playing worked beautifully. In Valentino's last film, *Son of the Sheik* (1926), Montague Love was introduced via this title: "Ghaba, the Moor, whose crimes outnumber the desert sands"— and proceeded to live up to that reputation via seven reels of lustful attentions to Vilma Banky. Ironically, although Miss Banky *was* raped during the film, it was by the hero!

The same year, Love played one of the screen's most despicable villains for Warner Brothers, in John Barrymore's *Don Juan*. As a cohort of Lucrezia and Cesare Borgia, Love played Count Donati, betrothed

Beery tries to explain wifely responsibilities to a reluctant Jetta Goudal in *The Coming of Amos* (1925).

of the lovely Adriana (Mary Astor) who, needless to say, has consented to the match only to save her father from death. The unsporting Donati, not content with trying to exercise his marital prerogative before the wedding, also manages to have Don Juan believe that the entirely innocent Adriana is Donati's mistress. And at the wedding feast, he further has the bad taste to stage a wild orgy and flirt outrageously with the nearly nude dancing girls! His bloody come-uppance in the film's famous duel sequence rightly drew cheers of approval.

The next year, Sam Goldwyn pitted him against Vilma Banky again in *Night of Love*. Right up his alley, this film built its premise around the medieval law of the *droit du seigneur*, whereby the lord of the manor could claim as his own bride, for one night, any maiden just married—literally snatching her from the altar. Love selects Ronald Colman's gypsy bride, and the indignity is too much for her. She commits suicide, whereupon Colman elects to get his vengeance in a like manner on Love's eventual bride—Vilma Banky. Veteran movie fans hardly need to be filled in any further on such a plot!

Noah Beery's silent villainy followed a similar course. Prior to 1920, while Montague was menacing Alice Brady, Noah (never as big a star as brother Wallace) was pursuing Mae Murray in *The Mormon Maid*. In the 1920's, he made both a wonderfully coarse and uncouth renegade in a series of Zane Grey westerns, and a cheerfully lecherous scoundrel in the DeMille production, *The Coming of Amos*. There, having tricked a White Russian princess into marriage, he is determined to exercise his rights. Kidnapping his bride (coolly beautiful Jetta Goudal), he takes her to his island fortress, and, leading her to the bedroom, tells her (via title of course): "Come, my dear, our nest is ready!" Outraged by the suggestion, his bride refuses, whereupon the resourceful Beery locks her in a cellar prepared for such emergencies, turns sundry locks and floodgates, and gradually fills the cellar with sea water. A further title tells her: "My last wife changed her mind down here!" Fortunately, Rod la Rocque arrives in time.

Beery enjoyed such roles to the hilt, but subtler villainy was well within his range. His Sergeant Lejaune in the silent *Beau Geste* was a fine characterization of a man who was a sadist and a killer, and yet at the same time a brilliant strategist and a courageous soldier. However, Beery seldom strayed so far from lecherous situations. He was back on familiar ground again in one of the best of the early talkies, 1929's *Isle of Lost Ships*. As the dictator of a colony of seamen shipwrecked in the Sargasso Sea, he carved nude figures in wood and tried a forced marriage to the

11

One of Beery's most famous roles: as Sergeant Lejaune, in *Beau Geste* (1926).

heroine, Virginia Valli. (In fairness to Beery and Love, it must be admitted that they were usually willing to try marriage first, reverting to force only when the heroine understandably demurred.)

The coming of sound all but put an end to their kind of villainy. The flamboyant adventure extravaganzas seemed to have no place in films which talked, and thus, unavoidably, seemed closer to reality. And in any case, wildly escapist yarns like *Night of Love* were considered out of place (as well as economically not feasible) in those grim Depression years. Love's

villainy was to be limited from now on, although his cultured English accent made him much in demand for playing both stiff-upper-lip officers and stuffed-shirt aristocrats. Beery, on the other hand, had a superbly fruity voice that matched exactly his jovial facial villainy. Obviously, he could not be put out to pasture. He played a singing buccaneer in the early all-talkie all-star musical revue *The Show of Shows*, and was then quickly taken up by the westerns and serials, where he remained an ace heavy until well into the 1940's.

As Count Donati, Montague Love breathes his last at the hands of John Barrymore in *Don Juan* (1926).

12

Beery rarely read a line just the way the script had it; invariably, he'd start off with a long grunt, a kind of verbal scowl, and wind up with twinkling eyes and a wicked chuckle, as though delighted at his own perfidy. In an early serial, *The Devil Horse*, his first scene has him riding up to a ranch, telling his men, "See if you can rustle up a few cattle!," and then burning the ranch down! A decade later, in another serial, *Zorro Rides Again*, he is told of an important shipment being made aboard a locomotive. His instant reaction to his henchman is a growled, "Can you get there in time *to wreck it?*" But it was at Paramount, in a series of Zane Grey westerns (many of them remakes of silents in which he had played the same villain roles), that he had his best sound opportunities, since the scripts invariably called for him to be beastly to his long-suffering wife or mistress (usually Blanche Frederici), while at the same time being excessively gallant (at first!) to the heroine. *Man of the Forest* has a classic moment in which, finally tired of playing the noble protector to the heroine, he determines to, as the old expression goes, have his way with her. His mistress tries to reason with him by calling on his loyalty. "I've been with you for twenty years," she tells him piteously.

"Well, you needn't count the last nineteen of 'em!" growls Noah before stalking out in search of Verna Hillie!

Both Noah Beery and Montague Love are gone now. Their great silent days are sometimes recalled for us on television. But, if the talking cinema never really did them justice, at least it achieved the coup de grâce of co-starring them, and giving them their heads in some old-time villainy. The film was *Out of Singapore*, and the fact that it was one of the cheapest of poverty-row quickies hardly matters. Noah and Montague ate it up, quite pushing the hero and heroine out of the picture. Noah was the master criminal, Montague his admiring lieutenant, sometimes hard put to it to believe that his mentor could be so resourceful. At one point, Noah, with becoming modesty, lists all the ways in which he has sunk ships and drowned crews for insurance, and beams that he has thought up an entirely new method. He tops this with the added information that he has very definite ideas as to what he will do with the heroine, whom he plans to abduct and take to a deserted island. The two scoundrels look at one another in mutual admiration, their eyes atwinkle with thoughts of the illegal delights to come. I'm sure that when director Charles Hutchinson shot that scene for a sixty-one minute quickie in 1932, he had no idea that he was creating one of the deathless moments of cinema!

Beery in a typically colorful villain characterization of the early twenties.

The lecherous glint in his eyes making no secret of his motives, Love struggles with Vilma Banky in 1927's *Night of Love*.

Beery was always having trouble with ladies who had fallen in love with him, and whom he had subsequently cast off. Miriam Seegar was his victim in *Out of Singapore*.

# THE BRUTES

Walter Long as Gus, the renegade, is sentenced following
a trial in the "invisible halls" of the Ku Klux Klan; from
*The Birth of a Nation* (1915).

The brute villains—facially ugly, physically powerful and almost invincible—human monsters who beat children, bully heroines, and mistreat animals, are represented throughout film history by a mere handful of great performers. This particular kind of villain has always been the most unsubtle of all in appearance, motivations, and characteristics, and thus has required extra subtlety in performance to prevent the character from becoming a mere stock cliché. The combination of brute strength, or at least the suggestion of it, with histrionic subtlety is not a combination one finds often on either stage or screen. Frequently, the brute strength is tempered by sentimentality—as with Victor McLaglen and Wallace Beery—or is indeed *all* that

Walter Long and Rudolph Valentino square off for a
fight to the death in *Moran of the Lady Letty* (1922).

Long, as Iron Head Joe, pursues Junior Coghlan along the yardarm in *The Yankee Clipper* (1927).

the player has to offer. Dick Sutherland, of the silents, was one of the ugliest brutes one could ever hope to find, and a useful villain in unambitious thrillers. But he was incapable of any kind of subtlety in his acting. In the talkies, Mike Mazurki, an ex-wrestler, a giant of a man with a thick, slow speech-delivery that effectively enhanced his standard role of slow-witted, murderous strong-arm man, likewise was too limited in acting ability to play anything other than psychopathic killers (as he did extremely well in *Murder, My Sweet*) or husky western villains (*Dakota*), albeit looking a bit out of place in the dandified outfit of a saloon keeper or gambler. One other villain in the talkies, Rondo Hatton, certainly fits into the "brute" category through a facial deformity that was rather tastelessly exploited in cheap horror films with titles like *The Brute Man*. Unfortunately, his literally Neanderthal face was accompanied by a listless acting style, and Hatton, who died some years ago, found himself

Donald Crisp as Battling Burrows in Griffith's *Broken Blossoms* (1919).

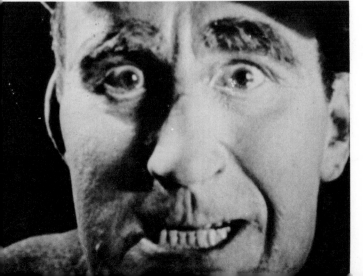

George Siegmann in *Merry-go-round* (1923).

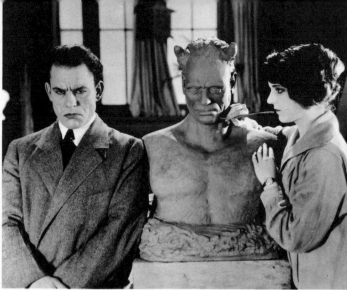

Lon Chaney, as a vengeance-crazed legless criminal, takes time out to answer Claire Adams' advertisement for an evil-looking man to pose for a bust of Satan! From *The Penalty* (1920).

almost in the "freak" category insofar as Hollywood was concerned.

Since the brute villains needed as much subtlety as they could muster, it is surprising that the foremost exponents of the art are to be found in the silent era, where such subtlety had to be attained solely through pantomime, without the aid of voice or dialogue.

Two of the all-time champs appeared together in 1915, in D. W. Griffith's *The Birth of a Nation*. Their names were Walter Long and George Siegmann. Walter Long played the renegade Negro, Gus, whose lust for Mae Marsh drives her to suicide. Long was a consummate actor whose muscular build and bull neck made him thoroughly convincing as a modern gangster, as a Hun, or as a Chinese warlord. His attacks on Mae Marsh in *The Birth of a Nation* and (as the small-time gangster) in *Intolerance* were terrifyingly convincing. Yet, when the subject matter was not so serious, when the aim was purely escapist adventure, he could play the same brute villain with tongue-in-cheek and pull off a richly florid performance. He brought this bravura approach to Cecil B. DeMille's *The Yankee Clipper*, a schoolboy-level sea adventure of 1927, in which he played, to quote his introductory title, "Iron Head Joe, mongrel whelp of the seven seas." Head shaven, a dagger in his belt, rings on his fingers and in his ears, he was a one-hundred-percent villain from the moment that he first laid lecherous eyes on the heroine as a sea breeze blew up her voluminous skirts! First, with false humility, he wheedles and whines; after a storm at sea in which most of the fresh water is lost, he brutally pushes the young cabin-boy out of the line for a cup of the precious water, and then beats a whining, smiling retreat as a bigger sailor puts him in his place; and, later, in the mutiny that he helped to formulate, he chases the

Ernest Torrence as the degenerate Luke Hatburn in *Tol'able David* (1921).

18

Gustav von Seyffertitz spent most of *Sparrows* (1926) trying to drown Mary Pickford and her brood of orphans in quicksand!

same cabin-boy up the rigging, dagger held between his gleaming teeth, as he joyfully pantomimes the carving-up process that is in store for the youngster—Junior Coghlan—when he is caught.

Long was popular with directors because he was easy and untemperamental to work with, and equally popular with leading ladies because he was such a

Tully Marshall as the crippled and perverted Baron Sadoja in *The Merry Widow* (1925), with Mae Murray.

charming fellow. He worked well into the sound era—his last films were in the 1940's—and he even played occasional straight and non-villain roles. But it was in the years from 1915 to 1926, or from *The Birth of a Nation*, with its serious brute, to *Eve's Leaves*, with its semi-comic Chinese warlord, that Long's finest portraits were created.

Like Long, George Siegmann was a D. W. Griffith player who got his first really important role in *The Birth of a Nation*. Siegmann had a huge bulk, hands that were like great bear-paws, and thin lips and cold eyes that he could utilize at will to suggest sadistic glee. In *The Birth of a Nation*, as a mulatto politician exploited by white carpet-baggers, he had a role that not only allowed him to whip helpless victims, beat a dog, and attempt to rape Lillian Gish, but also to be more than just a brute since the role, based largely on a known historical character who was a protégé of Thaddeus Stevens during the Reconstruction years, had considerable depth.

Siegmann also acted as an assistant director to Griffith on this and other films. He might well have become an important director had he, like Erich von Stroheim, Raoul Walsh, Tod Browning, W. S. Van Dyke and others of his contemporary assistants to Griffith, decided to concentrate on directing rather than acting. But he didn't, and a long gallery of some of the most vicious villains of the silent screen was the result. He was the tyrannical Cyrus the Persian in *Intolerance*, and in a third Griffith film, *Hearts of the World*, was the embodiment of the hateful Hun, even getting a second (and no more successful than the first) try at raping Lillian Gish. In William S. Hart's *Singer Jim McKee*, he was a sadistic keeper at a circus, deliberately mistreating the animals—and of course promptly set upon by Bill. But he outdid this unpleasantness with ease as one of the most disgusting of all the lecherous sadists created by director-writer Erich von Stroheim, in the 1923 film *Merry-go-round*. As

Walter James, a little-remembered brute-villain from the twenties.

the owner of a fairground concession in World War One Vienna, he takes a particular delight in brutalizing the helpless: an old man, a hunchback, his down-trodden wife (to whom he even doles out a single *thin* slice of salami as her sole evening meal!), and most especially the young heroine, played by Mary Philbin, whom he tries to rape on the darkened merry-go-round. And when her mother is dying upstairs, Sieg-mann, eyes glittering with lust, forces her to continue playing the hurdy-gurdy. Grinding his huge boot down on her slim foot, he commands her to "Smile!" through her grief and pain. Siegmann finally comes to a well-deserved end when he is torn asunder by an orangutan! *The Cat and the Canary* of 1927 saw him as a burly and terrifying guard from a lunatic asylum, helping to drive the heroine insane. And the very end of the silent era gave him a role that he had been born to play—the evil Simon Legree, in *Uncle Tom's Cabin*. An imaginative script (which twisted the original novel a bit, and brought the Civil War into it) height-ened the crimes of the already unspeakable Legree, and brought back echoes of Siegmann's *The Birth of a Nation* villainy. With his cheeks seemingly ruddy from the imbibing of too much liquor, and his lips and chin stained from tobacco juice, Siegmann made the almost stereotype-figure of Legree into one of the most real and terrifying movie villains of all.

The brutes like Legree who appeared first in plays or popular novels had of course a kind of built-in "depth" that helped them enormously. Audiences usually knew these villains ahead of time, and thus good actors like Siegmann were able to use that fore-knowledge to advantage by avoiding obvious bits of

William Nally and Pearl White in *Plunder* (1923).

20

character exposition. Another case in point is *Tol'able David*, the 1921 classic from a Joseph Hergesheimer novel. A story of mountain folk and old feuds, it provided Ernest Torrence with the villain role of his career as Luke Hatburn, the slobbering degenerate who kills and maims men and animals without a qualm. Torrence, a wonderful character actor and as effective a good guy as a bad guy, was an unmerciless scene-stealer, and nobody ever stood a chance against him—least of all in *Tol'able David*. His Luke Hatburn must surely rank among the most despicable villains of all time, and even Noah Beery, who played the role in the sound remake, couldn't top Torrence's performance.

"Battling Burrows," the villain of D. W. Griffith's *Broken Blossoms* (1919), was another brute deriving from a novel. In concept, the role of the prizefighter father who finally beats his child to death is one of the grimmest ever written. Donald Crisp's rather obvious playing of the role, contrasted with the delicate playing of Lillian Gish as his daughter, and Richard Barthelmess as her would-be lover, had to fall back on Griffith's subtitles for its subtleties, but it remains an impressive character, if not an overly impressive performance.

Erich von Stroheim's *Greed*, based on the Frank Norris novel *McTeague*, offered two strikingly contrasted screen brutes. Physically, Gibson Gowland, big-boned, curly-haired, awkward, clumsy, was ideal as the strong but kind and gentle McTeague, who becomes a brute and a murderer only when forced to it by the inhuman and degrading treatment afforded him by his wife (Zasu Pitts) whose mania for money

Jean Hersholt

Gibson Gowland bites wife ZaSu Pitts to force her to give him carfare; from Erich von Stroheim's *Greed* (1924).

21

Gibson Gowland and Jean Hersholt confront one another in Death Valley for the climax of *Greed*.

amounts to near-madness. As his rival and ultimate enemy, Jean Hersholt, as he was in so many silents, was a perfect example of the brute villain, less concerned usually with displaying his strength than with trying to acquire a veneer of sophistication. Hersholt's grease-smeared hair, loud shirts, and sullen scowl added vulgarity to his other defects. Seeing him as the hate-crazed rival in *Greed*, the bearded and burly killer in Mary Pickford's *Tess of the Storm Country*, the cheap and tasteless Ed Munn in the silent *Stella*

*Dallas*, or as the villain in that early talkie *Hell Harbor*, it is difficult to reconcile this human mònster with the roles he later played in talkies—the kindly Dr. Dafoe in the films with the Dionne Quints, or the Dr. Christian that indirectly came from it.

From Griffith came a logical successor to Walter Long in Louis Wolheim. Short, squat, ugly, Wolheim had contributed interesting minor villainies to such films as Barrymore's *Dr. Jekyll and Mr. Hyde*, and was the decidedly unsympathetic if not exactly vil-

Louis Wolheim with John Barrymore in *Dr. Jekyll & Mr. Hyde* (1920).

Wolheim directed as well as starred in *The Sin Ship* (1931) with Mary Astor.

lainous executioner in *Orphans of the Storm*. But as the real life scoundrel Captain Hare (the companion of Walter Butler in the Revolutionary War) in *America*, Wolheim came into his own as one of the foremost movie brutes. Hare was a sadist who used Mohawks and other Indian tribes in the war against the American rebels. He himself usually donned Indian warpaint so that he could join in the savage torture of victims. Wolheim has a chilling scene in *America* in which, obsessed with blood-lust, he tortures a captive and

gouges out his eyes. Wolheim's all-out villain roles were comparatively few, and he is of course far better remembered for his superb (and sympathetic) performance in *All Quiet on the Western Front*.

One looks in vain for the equal of Ernest Torrence, Jean Hersholt, or George Siegmann in sound films. When *Broken Blossoms*, *Tol'able David*, and *Tess of the Storm Country* were remade as talkies, their brute villains were much subdued. Henry Victor's circus strongman in *Freaks* was a character—

Anders Randolf attacks wife (Greta Garbo) and suspected lover (Lew Ayres) in *The Kiss* (1929).

Dudley Digges and Ann Harding in *Condemned* (1929).

Boris Karloff as Morgan, the dumb brute of a butler, goes on a drunken rampage and reaches out for Lillian Bond in *The Old Dark House* (1932).

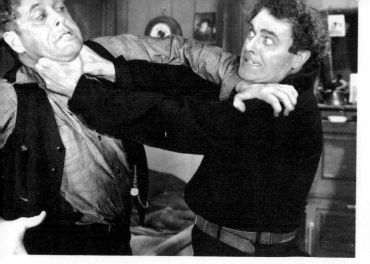

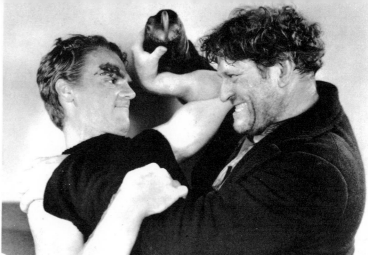

Ralph Ince, a veteran character actor and director, played a human monster in *Law of the Sea* (1932) and here receives last-reel justice from William Farnum.

Fred Kohler was rather unconvincingly beaten in this battle by the much smaller James Cagney: 1935's *The Frisco Kid.*

and a performance—somewhat in the old tradition, but that early talkie (1931) was actually so close in period and spirit to the silent era that one can hardly count it. Lon Chaney Jr.'s psychopathic brute in *Of Mice and Men* (1939) was an entirely different kind of character, and in any case not a villain. Other minor Chaney films tried to drag a certain brutishness into his villainy, but it was done solely to exploit his name and the memory of his Lennie in *Of Mice and Men.* Playing a standard western villain in *Frontier Badmen,* for example, he was given special billing as "Chango the Mad Killer," although Chango as it happened seemed to be no madder than Fred Kohler or Charles King had ever been, though possibly a trifle less educated.

Probably, just as the bravura swashbuckling villainy of Montague Love was considered passé, so was the uncomplicated brute. The talkies seemed to feel that if a villain behaved like a brute, there must be underlying reasons—and those reasons invariably resulted in his being played as a psychopath instead. This suspicion that the brute was considered "unrealistic" is bolstered by the fact that the only worthwhile talkie-era brutes turned up in that most unrealistic medium of all, the cartoon film. Disney's Pegleg Pete was the sound era's George Siegmann, and the Big Bad Wolf its Walter Long. Both of these crafty and powerful Disney villains had that little extra something, that touch of subtlety, that made them classic. On the other hand, Popeye's permanent enemy, and the eternal would-be seducer of Olive Oyl, the bearded and bloated Bluto, had nothing to offer outside of his strength and over-all repugnance. He was the talkies' equivalent of Dick Sutherland. Bluto was the villain in dozens of Popeye cartoons, yet is ignored and forgotten, and rightly so. The Big Bad Wolf was the villain in only two Disney cartoons, yet, like Long, Siegmann, and Torrence, he is with the immortals.

In a revamping of a silent Lon Chaney role, Walter Huston played "Deadlegs" Flint, paralyzed tyrant who rules an African domain from his wheel chair: *Kongo,* 1932.

Paul Hurst (second from right, in a scene from *Robin Hood of Eldorado*, 1936) had one of the meanest faces in movies. Seen at his best as a rapist, wartime looter, or lynch-mob leader!

One of the meanest and most brutish villains the movies ever gave us was Victor Jory's Injun Joe in 1938's *Adventures of Tom Sawyer*, seen here with Tommy Kelly in the spine-chilling sequence of the chase through the caves.

Alexandre Rignault, leading French contender for "brute" honors, with Jean Marais (left) in *L'Eternel Retour* (1942).

Rondo Hatton in *The Brute Man* (1946).

Dan Duryea as a new kind of forties' villain; the no-good or the pimp who slaps his women around, without the kind of virility that made it acceptable from Cagney and Gable in the thirties. With Joan Bennett in *Scarlet Street* (1945).

Ernest Borgnine, left, a throwback to the vicious bullies of Walter Long and Ernest Torrence until *Marty* humanized him. With Scott Brady and Ben Cooper in *Johnny Guitar* (1954).

# THE GOOD
# BADMAN

G. M. (Broncho Billy) Anderson, the very first good badman, in *The Girl from the Triple X*.

William S. Hart, prototype of all good badmen, as the outlaw who reforms in 1916's *Return of Draw Egan*.

The phrase "the good badman" became a cliché so early in the movies' development that even in 1916 Douglas Fairbanks used it as the title for one of his popular western spoofs! Considering the familiarity of the phrase, and the frequency which critics and historians have associated it with a hero-type of yester-year, it's surprising how few players ever really lived up to the description.

The first "good badman" was G. M. "Broncho" Billy Anderson, for the simple reason that he was also the first western star. Because he was setting all the precedents in his westerns from 1908 on, he didn't have to worry about breaking the rules, and cast himself as a sympathetic heavy quite as often as a more straightforward hero. Considering that Billy knew little about the West, his cowboy movies were surprisingly good—and the more he learned, the better they got.

But it is doubtful that the good badman as a type would have survived had it not been for William S. Hart, who came to westerns—already a mature man in his forties—in 1914. A former stage and Shakespearean actor, and a good one, Hart had been raised in the West. He loved the West and its history, and was determined to put it on the screen truthfully. And if Hart's "truth" was perhaps a little romanticized, it still had a rugged poetry and a stark austerity that no other western star or director (and Hart was both) has ever matched. Because he despised the dime-novel heroes, and because of his own sentimental streak, Hart frequently played an outlaw redeemed by love

29

Bill Elliott, another who emulated William S. Hart.

Realistically, they'd drink and smoke and carouse—but they'd never rat on a pal, abuse a child or ridicule the genuine word of God, regardless of their own lack of faith. Hart is too often dismissed (by those who have never seen him) as a strong, silent type, not to be taken seriously any more, who always came to a tragic end. Actually, Hart's screen deaths were few, and his films had a gutsy and realistic quality that commands serious attention and respect even today. He was the prototype of the good badman—and the best. (In the 1950's, however, Bill Elliott came surprisingly close to duplicating the Hart character in a series of intelligent "B" westerns for Monogram. Frequently playing the outlaw who reforms ( *Topeka* seems almost like a loose remake of Hart's *The Return of Draw Egan*), Elliott was however considerably less sentimental than Hart, and also less gallant. His westerner thought nothing of brutal third-degree methods to extract required information from helpless captives!)

There was a curious follow-up to Hart in the case of real-life badman Al Jennings, an Oklahoma train-robber who palled around with the James boys and the Daltons, but who was himself a rather inefficient bandit. So inefficient in fact that he was caught before his career was really under way, sent to prison, and pardoned some years later. What does a reformed train-robber do in 1919, when it isn't so easy to turn a dishonest dollar out West? Why, he enters the movies of course. Al Jennings made a whole series of two-reelers in the early 1920's, playing himself, with stories allegedly based on his exploits as a bandit. Of some sociological interest in that they did have a certain documentary value in reflecting the contemporary West, its customs and costumes, the films were of even more interest in that they showed real-life badman Jennings donning the mantle of movie badman Hart! Jennings, according to his movies, was a noble wanderer who righted wrongs, steered straying youngsters from the crooked path, saved the homes of widows, and prevented the bullying of dogs and orphans. Even a much whitewashed talkie movie version of Jennings' career, made in the 1950's with Dan Duryea as a Technicolor Al Jennings, didn't quite reach the "good badman" image that Al himself tried to create.

When streamlined cowboys Tom Mix and Ken Maynard took over, Hart's popularity waned, and the era of the good badman—in westerns at least—seemed to be over. But he was merely switching territories. He turned up again in the first of the big gangster movies, made in the late 1920's. George Bancroft, in Josef von Sternberg's *Underworld*, was an exact reincarnation of Hart—tough, fearing neither God nor man, yet with a code of nobility that finally causes him to lay down his life so that the girl he loves

—either of a woman, or a child. But there was nothing wishy-washy about Hart's reformations, and though he was usually gallant with the ladies, he also wasn't above taking what he wanted. In at least three of his westerns, he abducted the heroine and forcibly married her! But whether he was robber or killer, Hart's badmen usually lived by a rigorous and almost noble code.

Eddie Gribbon, Lew Cody and Victor McLaglen in *Not Exactly Gentlemen* (1931), a remake of the John Ford classic, *Three Bad Men.*

(Evelyn Brent) can marry the man she loves (Clive Brook).

But the Depression era knocked the romance out of most of the gang bosses, and, with the exception of Lew Ayres in *Doorway to Hell* (one of the best and most neglected early talkie gangster films), the new gangster heroes (if one can call them that) were without redeeming features. Once again the pendulum swung back to the West. Wallace Beery became the good badman of the sound era, an equivalent of Hart in a sense (though hardly his equal) but with major differences in approach. Hart's sentiment was delicate, underplayed, interwoven with such themes as brotherly love and conversion to a belief in God. Beery's sentiment was unadulterated slobber, often accompanied by facial mugging quite unworthy of such a good actor. Even his better films, such as *The Badman of Brimstone*, were afflicted with such overdone scenes as the *Stella Dallas* derivation where Beery watches his son's wedding. The son of course is unaware that Beery *is* his father, and Beery's presence there naturally causes his arrest.

One of the most poignant of the Hart films, *The Toll Gate*, had escaping outlaw Hart risk capture by stopping to save the life of a child. The sheriff, respecting this sacrifice, allows the outlaw (picturesquely named, like all Hart heroes; in this instance, "Black Deering") to escape to the border. The child's mother, a widow in love with Hart, wishes to go with him. But the outlaw, knowing that his life is not for a gentlewoman and a child, repudiates this chance for happiness, and rides off alone.

Beery's sentiment was never on such a mature or even romantic level. In an equivalent situation in a western of the 1940's, *Bad Bascomb*, Beery, on his way to safety, realizes that the child he has come to love (Margaret O'Brien) will be massacred in an Indian attack, and rides to bring the cavalry. The ride and the Indian attack are magnificent, only to be followed by the anticlimax of a maudlin and tearful farewell scene between the trembling tot and the bulky Beery, with the latter shamefaced at his own emotion as he tells her he'll be "all right," while the law is waiting in the wings to take him to the gallows. Only slightly less irritating were the comic-opera bandidos-with-a-heart-of-gold played by Leo Carrillo in *Flirting with Fate* and *The Gay Desperado*.

But other westerns of the sound era (one as recently as 1960) did have more authentic versions of the good badman. Randolph Scott in *Western Union* and *Ride the High Country* brought Hart's gradually reformed outlaw superbly back to life. And, curiously, there were excellent portrayals in three "B" westerns that are certainly worthy of note. *End of the Trail*, made by Columbia in the 1930's, had a literally shattering ending in which the hero (Jack Holt) is con-

Warner Baxter as Joaquin Murietta, romanticized into Mexico's *Robin Hood of El Dorado* (1936). America's outlaws, too, from Jesse James to Billy the Kid, have all been presented as both "good badmen" and even as completely upright heroes!

victed for the quite justifiable homicide of the villain. The sheriff, his friend (Guinn Williams), is unable to accompany him to the gallows. He sits in the jail, playing a sad little tune on a phonograph, while Holt walks to his death alone for the fadeout. A not dissimilar situation occurred in *Toll of the Desert*, a well-plotted if cheaply made poverty-row western, which

The comic-opera bandit with a heart of gold; Leo Carillo in *The Gay Desperado* (1936).

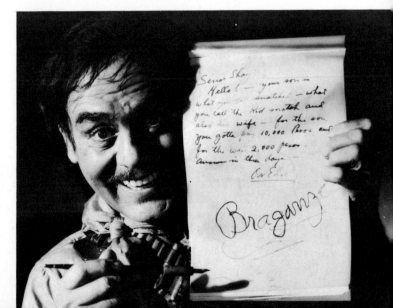

Cesar Romero was one of several (others were Kirk Douglas, Harry Carey and Victor Mature) to play Doc Holliday, the killer who palled up with Wyatt Earp. With Nancy Kelly in *Frontier Marshal* (1939).

reaches its climax with the hero (Fred Kohler Jr.) reluctantly hanging the outlaw-leader he has come to respect, not knowing that he is his own father. And, finally, in another rather crudely made independent western, *Arizona Badman*, the black-garbed badman of Edmund Cobb (a western hero in silent days, a straightforward villain and character player in sound films) is such a strong character, so completely drawing on the Hart prototype, that the film's nominal hero (Reb Russell) is quite overshadowed. For once, the heavy, who has such sure-fire sympathy-getting scenes as preventing another villain from shooting the hero in the back, and saving a crippled child from a beating at the hands of his bully of a father, has more actual footage than the hero, and is even allowed to escape scot-free at the end!

With *This Gun for Hire* (1942), it began to look as though we might be in for a return of the George Bancroft species of likeable gangsters. Alan Ladd's performance as Raven, the psychopathic yet sympathetic killer—kind to kittens and Veronica Lake—lifted him from a ten-year servitude in bits and minor roles, and made him a star overnight. But the rough, tough school of detective fiction was just around the corner. And America was at war. The gangster became a sadistic smoothie (and in the confused post-

Wallace Beery—a sugary 1930's equivalent of William S. Hart.

32

Beery in one of his most famous good badman roles: as Long John Silver, with Jackie Cooper, in 1934's *Treasure Island*.

Good badman James Cagney vs. all-in-black badman Humphrey Bogart in one of the most thoroughly enjoyable films of its type: *The Oklahoma Kid* (1939).

war years, a psychopath bothered by nightmares)—or he became a super patriot. Gangsters Alan Ladd in *Lucky Jordan* and Humphrey Bogart in *All Through the Night* suddenly discovered that they were first and foremost Americans, and applied gangster methods to the defeat of fifth column operations headed by Conrad Veidt and Peter Lorre. A lively little RKO thriller called *Seven Miles from Alcatraz* summed it all up. Two desperate cons escape from the rock, and hide out in a lighthouse, which is taken over by Nazis. In deciding to risk their own freedom by trying to outwit the Germans, one of the convicts explains it all very simply: "We may be rats, crooks, and murderers—but we're *Americans!*" And, in the postwar years, when the Communists supplanted the Nazis as the principal villains, one memorable moment had G-Man Edward G. Robinson appealing to the latent patriotism of gangster George Raft by listing his mistakes: "Murder . . . arson . . . blackmail . . . theft . . . those were all *petty* crimes, compared to what these people are planning!"

In this modern world, the subtle good badman has become so old-fashioned that I doubt if he'll reappear again, except possibly in the occasional reinvocation of William S. Hart. Nowadays, as long as a hoodlum is for America first, himself second, and communism not at all, he is automatically a "good badman."

George Bancroft, first of the tough but sympathetic gangsters; with Evelyn Brent in 1927's *Underworld.*

Last of the genuinely sympathetic gangsters: Alan Ladd in *This Gun For Hire* (1942).

# THE MASTER
# CRIMINALS

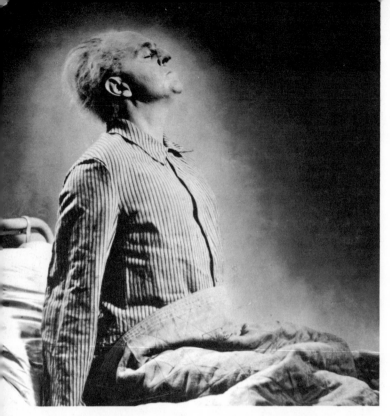

Greatest mastermind of them all—Rudolph Klein-Rogge as Dr. Mabuse, ruling an empire of crime from an insane asylum, in 1932's *The Testament of Dr. Mabuse*.

Here we are dealing not so much with a whole genre of criminals, but really with just five individual characters, each one of them such a genius of crime that the term "master criminal," loosely applied to any other well-organized but less God-like malefactor, seems almost an insult. Our five immortals, listed in

order of their appearance on the screen, are Professor Moriarty, perennial enemy of Sherlock Holmes; Dr. Mabuse, a hypnotist-criminal created by a German novelist, but actually brought to more spectacular life in a trilogy of films by director Fritz Lang; the wily Dr. Fu Manchu; Haghi, another Lang villain; and the more recent Dr. No. Note the preponderance of doctors and professors. They were all supremely cultured gentlemen, and the international scope of their activities, conducted more for power than mere monetary gain, inevitably lifted their film escapades from the realm of commonplace crime to that of worldwide espionage.

Spy melodramas, alas, are now as much a part of the past as Mary Pickford's *Rebecca of Sunnybrook Farm*, and, in view of today's political climate, are about as divorced from reality. The spy thriller reached its apex between the two world wars, when the nations of the earth were, comparatively speaking, peaceful and reasonably contented. The most serious upheavals seemed to be in Russia, and thus, not surprisingly, Russian agents tended to predominate in movie espionage. However, our "big five" were above politics themselves: either their organizations were so vast that it was to them, inevitably, that scheming nations came for help; or else they used the squabbling between nations to further their own ends! But all the ensuing espionage was on an adventurous rather than a political level. The great spy and crime organizations dealt in secret treaties and kidnapped diplomats on a plane so high that the individual was never affected. Few innocent bystanders ever got hurt either, except for those unfortunate passengers on sabotaged planes or trains, and, tactfully, the cameras never

Rudolph Klein-Rogge as another classic Fritz Lang criminal: Haghi, in *Spies* (1928).

Examples of the colorful and bizarre underlings that carried out the orders of Lang's super-criminals: at right, thugs supervise the work of blind counterfeiters in *Dr. Mabuse* (1922); center and bottom, two of the Nazis working undercover in England in *Manhunt* (1941).

lingered on such carnage. Espionage was a game as much as it was a crime, a game played without serious consequences. When one faction lost out, the defeated spy was usually sportsman enough to doff his hat to his opponent, and, like Paul Lukas in *The Lady Vanishes*, wish him "jolly good luck." Spying became more serious after World War Two, and was soon so inextricably entangled with politicians and the military (*Night People, Diplomatic Courier*—both now frighteningly old-hat after only a few years) that it was just no longer fun. Now the happy days of secret treaties and "complications" in the Balkans are gone forever; with nuclear warfare an ever-present threat, the individual is very much involved, and diplomats just aren't worth kidnapping any more.

By later standards, Conan Doyle's arch-villain, Professor Moriarty, seems almost unambitious. His activities were worldwide, but only because it would have been too boring to limit his crimes to England. His ultimate aims were never made too clear, and, despite his myriads of agents and magnificently coordinated organization, he seemed to plan only for the moment—and principally to confound Sherlock Holmes. Unlike his successors, he was unbusiness-like enough to do much of his dirty work himself. Delighting in bizarre disguises, he would frequently confront Holmes, who, sportsman to the end, made no move to overpower his enemy physically, and preferred to wait and plot some equally involved counter-strategy. The silent *Sherlock Holmes* of 1922 gave us one of the best Moriartys of all in Satanic-featured Gustav von Seyffertitz. Barrymore, whose classic profile made a splendid contrast with Gustav's, used von Seyffertitz as his villain more than once, and, in both *Sherlock Holmes* and *Don Juan* contrived sequences in which, by distorting his features, he masqueraded—convincingly—as his evil opponent.

The sound Holmes films brought many more Moriartys to the screen. Ernest Torrence essayed the role in an early American talkie, while Lynn Harding played Moriarty to Arthur Wontner's Holmes in some British adventures. And, from 1939 through the early 1940's, there was a veritable parade of alternating Moriartys to Basil Rathbone's Holmes. George Zucco was the first, followed by Lionel Atwill, and Henry Daniell—all three playing the role with relish.

While the screen's interpretations of Professor Moriarty were reasonably faithful to Doyle's original conception, Sax Rohmer's Dr. Fu Manchu was somewhat short-changed both by a British studio in the

Paul Lukas (right) was the master spy in Alfred Hitchcock's *The Lady Vanishes* (1938) with Michael Redgrave, Margaret Lockwood.

Gustav von Seyffertitz as Moriarty opposite John Barrymore in *Sherlock Holmes* (1922).

1920's (which made a series of featurettes built around the character) and by Hollywood. Rohmer's insidious doctor was, for all his unspeakable tortures and chain-murders, not entirely unsympathetic. His motives were more respectable than his methods, he followed a definite code of honor, could be quite sportsman-like at times, and, above all, was possessed of a giant intellect that invariably caused him to triumph over the forces of law and order in the larger sense, even though his particular scheme of the moment might have been forestalled by the redoubtable Nayland Smith. The movies, however, capitalized only on his colorful blood-lust and genius for torture.

Warner Oland made his Fu Manchu films in that unfortunate period of the change-over to sound. Rohmer's lightning-paced stories required a tempo and steadily building tension that the static adaptations of 1929 lacked quite deplorably. In any case, Oland, although an excellent actor, had been too steeped in Oriental villainy for years for his new role

38

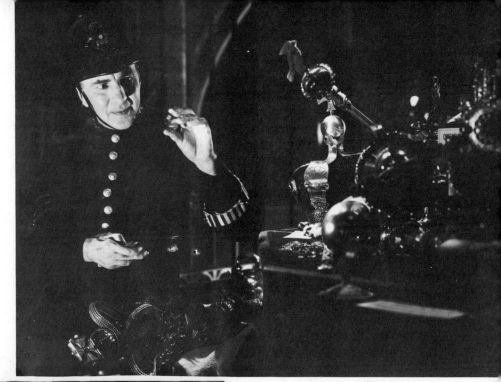

A later Moriarty, George Zucco, robs the Crown Jewels from the Tower of London in *Adventures of Sherlock Holmes* (1939).

George Zucco and Henry Daniell, who both played Moriarty, gang up on Holmes (Basil Rathbone) *together* in *Sherlock Holmes in Washington* (1942). The third villain, extreme right, is Bradley Page.

to be anything more than an extension of his earlier performances.

In 1932 the movies found its best Fu Manchu in Boris Karloff, via MGM's *The Mask of Fu Manchu*. Physically an ideal choice, Karloff was able to make the doctor an intelligent as well as a sinister villain, and to suggest something of the ageless quality of the Fu Manchu of the books. However, grand and glorious hokum though it was, the film reduced Fu's international omnipotence to a mere serial-like procession of

lurid thrills and fantastically elaborate torture devices, including a giant bell, a huge press lined with spikes, and a seesaw (controlled by sand, on an hour-glass principle) that gradually lowered its victim to ravenous crocodiles. The doctor's operating room was curiously and carelessly kept, with pythons, venomous spiders, scorpions, and other "donors" to a mysterious serum slithering quite happily in and out of their quite inadequate jars. Fah Lo Suee, Fu's sensual daughter (quite a complex and likeable character in the books),

became a gloriously psychopathic nymphomaniac in Myrna Loy's bejewelled hands. Fu's only and frequently repeated modus operandi was to "wipe the whole accursed white race from the face of the earth," and the reward for his legions of followers was to be to "kill all the white men and mate with their women." However, his lack of esteem for the whites was in some ways understandable, since Lewis Stone, as Scotland Yard's Sir Nayland Smith, strode through the film muttering jingoistic remarks about "superstitious Oriental heathens," and calling his always polite opponent a "yellow monster" on the least provocation. In the film's climax, Sir Nayland turns an electrical death-ray loose, calmly mowing down hundreds of Orientals—and leaving it running at full blast for the benefit of any other Chinese who might accidentally stumble into its path! However, in its simple, unrestrained way, and with its magnificently overblown dialogue, *The Mask of Fu Manchu* is a classic of its kind, and, regardless, of script unsubtleties in the conception of Fu himself, Karloff was the ideal choice for the role.

Thereafter, the Chinese mastermind was absent from the screen until the 1940's, when Henry Brandon

Subjecting Lawrence Grant to the "bell torture," Fu Manchu (Boris Karloff) tries to elicit information about the newly discovered tomb of Genghis Khan, in *The Mask of Fu Manchu* (1932).

40

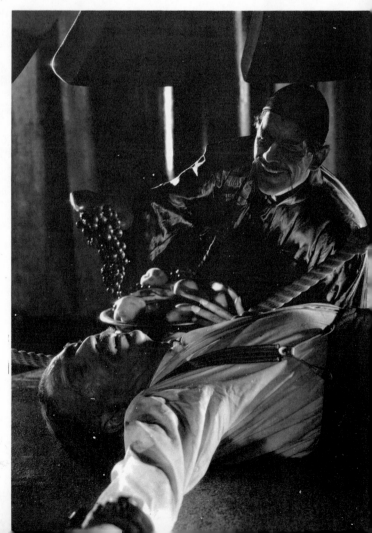

played the role surprisingly well in a serial, *The Drums of Fu Manchu*, which succeeded rather nicely in remaining true to the spirit of Rohmer's novels. A cheap television series that followed is beneath contempt and need not be discussed here, except to add that a pilot for the series—directed by William Cameron Menzies, with John Carradine as Fu Manchu and Cedric Hardwicke as Sir Nayland Smith, was quite superior to the lackluster series that ultimately followed, with Glenn Gordon making a singularly inept Fu Manchu.

Fritz Lang's Dr. Mabuse made his first appearance in 1922, a criminal and a counterfeiter (employing an army of blind technicians to operate his forging plant) who was also a super-hypnotist. His favorite stunt was to mesmerize his victims into committing suicide, usually by driving their cars off the cliffs of a quarry. The first *Dr. Mabuse*, a silent, was a bizarre but rather rambling affair, held together primarily by the spellbinding personality of Rudolph Klein-Rogge, Lang's favorite villain, and a sort of German forerunner of Karloff and Chaney.

A later Lang German film, *Spies* (1928), gave to Klein-Rogge what was really an extension of and improvement on the Mabuse film. Living a triple life as a master spy, an eminent banker, and a vaudeville clown, this criminal, Haghi, was seemingly omnipotent as he kept several steps ahead of the Russian, Japanese, German, and English secret services, stole treaties, assassinated diplomats, collected huge sums from banks via forged checks signed in disappearing ink, operated a radio network, and thought nothing of wrecking the Paris express just to eliminate one man! His men were everywhere, and apparently prepared for *every* emergency. At one point, a car chase, which couldn't have been predicted, is terminated when a Haghi minion, posing as a street fruit-vendor, heaves coconuts at the police. The coconuts turn out to be gas bombs! Mabuse and Haghi both delight in crime for its own sake and for the power it gives them; both being exceptionally brilliant men could doubtless have achieved that same power by quite legal means had they been so inclined. But, unlike Fu Manchu, who always triumphed in the end, they always met defeat—not so much through the efforts of the police, always presented by Lang as rather dull, plodding, and quite colorless officials, as through their own ambition and genius leading them into insanity. Haghi comes to a truly spectacular end in *Spies* when his identity is discovered while he is doing his clown

act at the vaudeville theater. His rather macabre act consists of shooting at oversized models of roaches, flies, and spiders. Seeing the police closing in on him, he goes insane, fires point-blank into his head, and then laughs fiendishly at the audience while telling the stage hands to ring down the curtain. The audience laughs and applauds vociferously at what it imagines to be just a part of the act.

Lang's *The Testament of Dr. Mabuse* of 1931 pulled off the near-impossible by being better than either of its predecessors, and one of the most gripping thrillers ever made. Here, the insane Mabuse—still played by the magnificent Klein-Rogge—is conducting his huge crime organization from an asylum, by hypnotizing the director of the asylum into carrying out his orders. (Curiously, this situation had a real-life counterpart in Germany in the 1950's, when a madman who proved to have a genius for organization, hypnotized an associate into obtaining money by forgery and other crimes. When the hypnotist was finally captured, he boasted that his spoils were going toward

A cut scene from *The Mask of Fu Manchu*. In final form, it was Jean Hersholt (not Lewis Stone, above) who was strapped to this device—on the theory that it looked more frightening for a fatter man to be impaled!

Henry Brandon as the Oriental genius in *Drums of Fu Manchu* (1941), with victim Philip Ahn and dacoit-slave John Merton.

the establishment of his own organization of crime!) Mabuse dies, but his spirit takes over the mind and body of the asylum director, and the brilliantly conceived crimes go on. The purpose of the crimes this time is not wealth or even power, but the need "to throw mankind into an abyss of terror" so that, from the confusion and chaos, a new order can take over. Reputedly worried by this forewarning of Nazi methods (although it is doubtful that the German populace as a whole would have seen the parallel) and by the imparting of Nazi slogans and methods to a lunatic, Dr. Goebbles called Lang on the carpet, and banned the film. Lang escaped to France, taking a print of the film with him. *The Last Testament of Dr. Mabuse* came to its end as had the two predecessors: Mabuse, or Professor Baum as he now is, retreats once more into insanity.

As far as Lang was concerned, that was the end of his Doctor Mabuse. But, in the early 1960's, returning to Germany, he was persuaded to make one more film in the series. The result was *The Thousand Eyes of Dr. Mabuse*, in which a new master-criminal, a disciple of Mabuse, trying to create the impression that Mabuse is still alive, emulates his methods in contemporary Germany, with atomic secrets as some of the stakes. The "thousand eyes" were secret television sets that enabled the new Mabuse to spy on all the guests in a deluxe hotel. It was to be expected that it would fall short of the three originals; but, for a film made in the 1960's by a man in his seventies, it had astonishing vigor and imagination. Mabuse suddenly became a box office name again, and several other Mabuse films went into production—but none of them were made by Lang, who had now finished with his arch-villain once and for all, and none of them of course could hold a candle to that old maestro, Rudolph Klein-Rogge.

Our fifth mastermind, Dr. No, arrived on the

scene in 1962 as the nuclear age's equivalent of Dr. Mabuse. His worldwide organization was as efficiently organized as Mabuse's; his intellect challenged that of Fu Manchu. If he seemed to have an unfair advantage in that so much of his efficiency derived from up-to-date scientific marvels, radar, nuclear reactors, etc., it was to a degree counterbalanced by the fact that the law now had the use of similar electronic brains, and that his opponent, secret serviceman James Bond, went about his work secure in the knowledge that he had a "permit" to kill whenever he felt justified. Fallen enemies on either side in *Dr. No* get little pity, and are calmly killed out of hand— something that Sherlock Holmes, Sir Nayland Smith, and Inspector Lohmann would never have dreamed of doing.

Dr. No, equipped with the same kind of black-gloved artificial hand that Klein-Rogge had once utilized in *Metropolis*, did get his apparently "final" come-uppance at the end of his first adventure. But it seems likely that author Ian Fleming will see fit to revive him in due time. After all, 1964 has brought Dr. Mabuse back to the screen. Billy Wilder announces that Sherlock Holmes and Moriarty will be back. MGM is remaking *The Mask of Fu Manchu*. His one tentative stab at world domination doesn't really raise Dr. No to the social level of Fu or Dr. Mabuse, but nevertheless he has come closer than anyone else to challenging their crown. Who knows, just as the Frankenstein Monster, Dracula, and the Wolf Man were co-starred in the early 1940's, perhaps someone will have the bright idea of aligning Dr. Mabuse, Fu Manchu, Professor Moriarty, Haghi, and Dr. No in one mighty syndicate of world crime! Then we would indeed have the crime thriller to end them all!

The last (to date) of the screen's criminal masterminds: Joseph Wiseman, left, in the title role of *Dr. No* (1963) with (center) Sean Connery and Ursula Andress.

# THE WESTERN
## OUTLAWS

Robert Kortman, with William Desmond and Enid Markey, in *Lieut. Danny, USA* (1916).

No other single group of pictures has ever produced such a colorful, varied, and spectacularly prodigious group of villains as the good old horse opera. To illustrate them all, and catalog their various special vices, would take a volume in itself. And the field is further complicated by the number of western stars who, in later years; switched from hero to villain roles. Bob Steele, Kermit Maynard, Lane Chandler, Edmund Cobb, Wally Wales, Jack Perrin, Tom Tyler, Bob Livingston, Tom Keene, and (once only) even Buck Jones are among the erstwhile sagebrush cavaliers who doubtless caused the shedding of many juvenile tears when they transferred to the wrong side of the law. To further muddy the waters, many

Two decades later, Robert Kortman in *Swifty*, menacing Hoot Gibson and June Gale.

Wheeler Oakman (with neckerchief), William Farnum and Kathryn Williams in the first version of *The Spoilers* (1914).

western stars on occasion played dual roles, as hero *and* villain. In the long run, perhaps, the villains were even better known (by sight, if not by name) than the heroes. A cowboy star such as Charles Starrett or Gene Autry could make at most eight movies a year; but a villain such as Dick Curtis or Roy Barcroft was not so limited, and could (and often did) appear in twenty or more movies within the same year!

From the 1920's on, the western villain has fallen largely into one of two camps. There have been the well-groomed masterminds, intellectual rather than physical types, usually much smarter than the hero who wins out by luck and the fact that "right" is on his side. And, secondly, there have been the roughnecks—villains for whom complicated legal chicanery is too much of a strain, and who settle for rustling a few cows instead of land-grabbing. Of course, the hoodlum-villains also serve their purpose as henchmen for the masterminds, and as convenient punching-bags for the heroes. To these two basic groups, we might also add two runner-up groups. Since the West inevitably invites get-rich-quick speculators from the East, western movies have been able to utilize such "dude" villains as Warner Oland, Warren William, John Miljan, John Carradine, Brian Donlevy, Lee J. Cobb, Herbert Rawlinson, Kenneth Harlan, and Robert Frazer, some of them former top-liners of the silent screen, and all of them good enough actors to take on any one of the stock roles, good guy or bad, of western movies—town banker, sheriff, railroad surveyor, stageline operator, cattle owner, or heroine's father. Even horror-specialist Lionel Atwill left his

laboratory long enough to play the villain in a western serial, and, in later years, with the Nazis and then the Communists transferring their operations to the Western ranges, there was further opportunity for facial and racial variety.

But it took many years for the western badmen to become to diversified. The early one-reel westerns

Alfred Hollingsworth and William S. Hart in *Hell's Hinges* (1916).

45

Louise Glaum, Robert McKim, William S. Hart in *The Return of Draw Egan* (1916).

Luella Maxim, William Desmond and Ed Brady in *Deuce Duncan* (1918).

James Mason, extreme left, with Douglas Fairbanks in *Knicker-bocker Buckaroo* (1918).

produced by D. W. Griffith and Thomas Ince created few villain-types for the reason that in those pre-star-system days, there was little or no type-casting. Harry Carey would play an honest sheriff in one western, a badman in the next. And the same was true of Henry B. Walthall, Tom Chatterton, Francis Ford, and others in the Griffith and Ince stock companies.

The first recognizable villain type began to emerge in 1914, with Tom Santschi's McNamara in the first version of *The Spoilers*, and in the films of William S. Hart. Drinking and smoking didn't stamp him as a heavy right away (as it would in later years) because the western *hero* of those years was a realistic figure who drank and smoked too. But the heavy would usually chomp on a *cigar*, as a kind of status symbol of ill-gotten affluence, while the honest hero would roll his own. Since many of the early westerns, and especially those of Thomas Ince, simplified the good-vs.-evil struggle by pitting the church against the saloon, the flowery waistcoats, clean boots, or long black frock-coat of the saloon-owner of themselves became implied symbols of evil. The basic vices of the villain in this period were not so much greed or dishonesty or lust, but just plain orneriness. Villains such as Frank Campeau, Sam de Grasse, James Mason, Bob Kortman, and Robert McKim were slim, rangy individuals, untidy, seedy-looking opportunists, usually out for the quick dishonest dollar, and comparatively unambitious compared with later villainous brethren. They scowled and sneered perpetually, and were usu-

Villainous and unshaven animal trainers were frequent heavies in silent westerns. In Tom Mix's *The Circus Ace* (1927) the bad guy was Stanley Blystone, whose brother John was one of the best directors of Mix westerns.

Western train robber Al Jennings, who turned to movies in 1919.

ally introduced to the audience with an act that illustrated their perfidy right away. More than one Hart villain was seen beating a boy or a dog in his first scene. When Douglas Fairbanks introduced Sam de Grasse in *Wild and Woolly* (another Fairbanks spoof of westerns, while still being an exciting specimen in its own right), he made the audience detest him instantly by having him stub out a lighted cigar on the hand of an Indian servant! If these devices sound unsubtle, it shouldn't be assumed that such villains were hard to believe in. After all, there are probably far more real-life villains who get drunk and mistreat dogs than there are polished scoundrels of the Sydney Greenstreet variety. Many of the mean-looking villains of these pre-1920 westerns, Bob Kortman, Ed Brady, Leo Willis, were still plying their trade more than twenty

Dan Duryea, left (with John Dehner), playing Jennings on the screen in *Al Jennings of Oklahoma* (1951). Al lived to see, and presumably enjoy, this version of his career.

Robert Taylor as Billy the Kid (1941); Brian Donlevy, normally a villain, plays lawman Pat Garrett.

48

years later, age merely having enhanced their disreputable appearance.

The charm of all these fellows was that, unlike the later and far more business-like villains, they were mean merely for the sheer joy of being mean, and because they carried a "hate" for the hero that could never be slated. The heavy in *The Testing Block* for example, contrives to have William S. Hart jailed, and then, through the cell window, tells Hart that he is literally going to ride Hart's beloved pinto pony to death, after which he plans to abduct Hart's wife. As an after-thought, he adds the information that Hart's child is near death.

Such inspired villainy became rare on the screen after western heavies found themselves neatly cataloged as "rustlers," "claim-jumpers," or what have you, although Tom Tyler's vicious Luke Plummer in John Ford's *Stagecoach* of 1939 was an invigorating return to the old manner.

Noah Beery and a colorful imitator, Alfred Hollingsworth, held up the more flamboyant side of movie villainy in early (pre-1920) westerns, but it was the success of *The Covered Wagon* (1923) and *The Iron Horse* (1924), the first two really big western epics, that prompted the wholesale development of a new crop of heavies. Overnight, westerns—big and small—became big business, and the mass production boom was on. In the 1930's, almost every company had two or three western series going simultaneously (the average series offered eight per year), and literally hundreds of assembly-line westerns were offered every year. Under such a modus operandi, it is not sur-

Another of the endless Billy the Kid sagas: Audie Murphy and Albert Dekker in *The Kid from Texas* (1949).

In *The Outlaw* (1943), Billy the Kid (Jack Beutel) had sex on his mind far more than the bandit business. With Walter Huston and Jane Russell.

49

In *The Painted Desert* (1930), a pre-Hopalong William Boyd corners a pre-Rhett Butler Clark Gable.

That same year, before his success as the Frankenstein monster, Boris Karloff still played an occasional western heavy: with Dorothy Sebastien, Rex Lease and, at right, old reliable Tom Santschi in *The Utah Kid*.

prising that there wasn't too much depth of characterization in the western heavy of the 1930's and 1940's. The best of them, Fred Kohler, Walter Miller, LeRoy Mason, Charles King, Harry Woods, were holdovers from the 1920's. Some of them had been former heroes, and thus broke tradition a little as heavies in being either handsome (as in the case of LeRoy Mason) or at least distinguished (Harry Woods and Walter Miller). Curiously, television later reversed this trend. In its search for the "offbeat" and the "adult," it often took the unheroic faces of former movie villains (Tristram Coffin, Barton MacLane) and made them upright if unglamorous lawmen!

Round-faced, black-mustached Charles King rapidly became the apotheosis of all western villains. Equally at home playing the "big boss" in tailored suit, or the lowly unshaven minion in torn and dirty jeans, he was successively pulverized in climactic fist fights by every western star in the business, from Ken Maynard and Buck Jones through Tex Ritter, Gene

The western continued to be a useful training ground: 1942's *Hoppy Serves a Writ* shows Robert Mitchum as one of the badmen cowed by William Boyd.

John Wayne coming to grips with Yakima Canutt in *The Lucky Texan* (1934).

Autry, Johnny Mack Brown, and even Lash LaRue! Few non-western aficionados knew his name, but almost any moviegoer would identify him as "Blackie"—the semi-symbolic name he invariably used.

LeRoy Mason was almost as well-known. Perhaps his greatest moment of glory occurred in a late chapter of a Republic serial, *The Painted Stallion*. Engaged in a gun battle on a rocky ledge, his gang is rapidly being decimated by the hero's withering fire. A henchman begs him to withdraw because they're losing too many men. "That's O.K.," replies Mason nonchalantly, "I've got lots of men!"

The 1930's were full of lovably mean faces. Stuntman Yakima Canutt was much in demand for his amazing leaps, wagon crashes, and horse falls. He not only played villains, but doubled for the hero (especially for John Wayne, in an early Monogram series) and thus, through astute editing, was often quite literally chasing himself. Dick Curtis and Dick Cramer both looked too evil to be true. Tom London and Bud

Osborne, veterans from the earliest days of the movies, continued to ride and fight into their seventies, and both died in harness in early 1964. Roy Barcroft, deliberately patterning himself on Harry Woods, menaced all the Republic heroes in the 1940's and 1950's. And there were John Merton, Kenneth Mc-Donald, Dick Alexander, Jack Rockwell, Ernie Adams, and scores of others. The list became even more endless in the late 1940's, when many of the old crop of villains began to retire, or to move to quieter and less

An almost unbeatable trio of heavies: Harry Woods, Roy Barcroft and Robert Frazier in *Dawn on the Great Divide* (1942).

An equally classic group from De-Mille's *The Plainsman* (1936): Richard Alexander, James Mason, Fred Kohler, Charles Bickford.

William Boyd catches up with Francis MacDonald and Willard Robertson in *Range War* (1939).

Indians as the stock fire-water befuddled villains, in *Wild and Woolly* (1917).

Fred Kohler with Tom Mix in *The Fourth Horseman* (1933).

strenuous character roles, and the roster took on new, younger names—Marshall Reed, Lane Bradford, Holly Bane, Myron Healey—none of whom ever really looked quite at home in their western clothing, and none of whom certainly achieved immortality in their particular niche.

If I were ever asked to nominate the best western badman of all, I don't think there would be much of a mental struggle before Fred Kohler's name was elevated to that lofty pedestal. Fred was a badman of the old school—crafty, ugly, brawny, happier with the

Harry Shannon, Gregory Peck and Richard Jaeckel in one of the most intelligent of westerns, *The Gunfighter* (1950).

Jack Palance as the sadistic killer who makes war on the farmers in George Stevens' classic *Shane* (1951); about to "get his" is Elisha Cook, Jr.

Stuntmen Cliff Lyons (left) and Fred Graham hold John Wayne, while Mike Mazurki hovers uncertainly in the background: *Dakota*, 1945.

J. P. McGowan, Tom London and Gene Autry in *Guns and Guitars* (1936).

Most of the movie gangsters—Cagney, Bogart *et al.*—took their crime out West eventually. Richard Widmark's first (but far from last) essay in western villainy was in *Yellow Sky* (1948).

Johnny Mack Brown and Dick Alexander

John Wayne and Leroy Mason

Ken Maynard and Charles King

Buck Jones and Charles King

Bob Steele and Bud Osborne

Leon Ames

John Merton

Stanford Jolley

Walter Miller

Karl Hackett

Monte Blue

Chief Thundercloud

Morris Ankrum

Iron Eyes Cody

Kenneth MacDonald

Brian Donlevy

Bud Osborne

Jack Ingram

Marshall Reed

simple villainies of robbing stagecoaches or rustling cattle, and not one to have others do his dirty work for him. When displeased, which was frequently, he'd grind his teeth audibly and glower. Hardly a flashy dresser, he'd add vulgarity to bad taste by wearing an obnoxiously stiped shirt without its collar and tie. His meanest crime was probably hacking an old man to death with a tomahawk—and blaming the Indians. The closest he ever got to grandeur was when, as an agent of Russia, he tried to capture California for them in the serial *The Vigilantes Are Coming*. His only brush with culture was the installation of an organ in his mountain hideaway in *Honor of the Range*—an organ the heroine promptly proceeded to play to summon the aid of Ken Maynard in saving her from the proverbial fate worse than death. And in Fred's huge paws, who knows, it might well have been!

Fred Kohler vigorously plied his villainy in big westerns and small, from DeMille's *The Plainsman* to a Roy Rogers "B." In 1924, he and George O'Brien were mortal opponents in one of the biggest of all spectacular western epics, John Ford's *The Iron Horse*. Fourteen years later, these two husky he-men were still trading insults and punches in a much less elaborate but no less expert "little" western, *Lawless Valley*. But something else had been added. Fred Kohler Jr., every bit as mean and brawny as his old man, was by then an up-and-coming western villain too, and in *Lawless Valley* he played the son of Fred Sr.! At one point, the conniving pair disagree on the correct procedure for a particularly reprehensible piece of skullduggery, and Fred Jr. protests, "Aw, that's crazy!" That familiar scowl comes to Fred Sr.'s face, and he growls back "Careful son, you're talking to your dad, you know!"

# THE FOREIGNERS

*Border Incident* (1949) maintains the tradition with two of the scurviest Mexican villains ever, Alfonso Bedoya and Arnold Moss (center), but makes it "all right" by having them in the pay of American racketeer Howard da Silva.

Hollywood, from its earliest days up until the general "housecleaning" in 1934, had never had any qualms at all about using racial and minority groups for comedy purposes. Race, religion, sex, mental sickness, physical deformity, occupation—nothing was sacred. Sometimes tastelessly, but usually with wit and a genuine spirit of fun, Hollywood poked fun at Greeks, Negroes, Jews—and ministers, homosexuals, kings, presidents, and street-cleaners—all with impunity. Every Jew had a scraggly beard and was forever after the dollar. Every Italian was a "wop," and, automatically, a barber or a boot-black. It was a free and easy period in which very real racial insults were happily ignored, as opposed to today's rather more tense state of affairs when possible or potential racial insults can cause wholesale stoppages of work, riots, and newspaper crusades. But in the 1920's particularly, nobody really complained. After all, when everybody is being maligned, who is actually being discriminated against? American movies were full of outrageously caricatured "Limeys," and the British, instead of getting peeved, merely put outrageously caricatured "Yanks" into their movies.

None of the races seemed to mind being ridiculed

The last days of the "Yellow Peril"; Edward G. Robinson, Lupe Velez, Lew Ayres and Henry Kolker in *East is West*.

61

Tully Marshall, J. Carrol Naish, Noel Madison and Edward G. Robinson in *The Hatchet Man* (1932), a tale of tong wars and Chinese gangsters in Frisco of the late twenties.

far beyond the point of normal satire. It was all right that they be depicted as oafs, incompetents, and pompous fools. But there was, apparently, one serious note of dissention. It was *not* all right to suggest that their particular race had characteristics suiting them for criminal pursuits!

The Mexicans were the first to complain—bitterly —that they were being ill-used in Hollywood westerns. And it's true that many an early western depicted the Mexican as swarthy, lecherous, treacherous, and murderous—more given to a knife in the dark than an honest shoot-out in the streets at high noon. The Mexi-

can made a particularly convenient villain, too, since his geographic proximity to American states made his marauding on this side of the border quite logical. Too, his standard sombrero and colorful costuming made him stand out from the American cowboy, and in the fight and chase scenes made the division of good guys and bad guys easily apparent. And, since Pancho Villa was so much in the news at a time when the westerns of Bill Hart and others were really getting up steam, and had himself led bandit raids into American territory, the Mexican villain was not only convenient but logical—just as the German or Japanese villain became

Marlene Dietrich as a notorious China "coaster," Clive Brook as a somewhat stuffy British officer, and Warner Oland as Chang, the warlord, in *Shanghai Express* (1932). The dialogue left little doubt as to Hollywood's convictions on the inferiority of all Orientals!

*Scarface* (1932) suggested that all gangsters were Italians and that their key aims in life were expensive clothes—and expensive *American* women. Osgood Perkins, mistress Karen Morley and upcoming gangster Paul Muni sampling the merchandise before taking it over.

a matter of course in wartime. Even when a western didn't use a Mexican villain, it often took pains to point out that the Texan or Arizonan badman was as bad as a Mexican. *Hell's Hinges*, one of William S. Hart's 1916 westerns, introduced the 100% American villain (Alfred Hollingsworth) with a title explaining that he "combined the deadly cunning of the rattlesnake with the oily craftiness of the Mexican." The point was not so much that Mexicans were always used as villains—actually the percentage of Mexican as opposed to American villains was fairly small—but it is true that whenever a Mexican was used at all, it was

invariably as the villain. Finally, official protests to the American government had their results. President Wilson intervened, and asked the movie-men to please be a little kinder to the Mexicans. And the movie-men complied. After all, they still had the Indians, who were certainly 100% American, and not strong enough to protest.

In later years, Germany, which made many authentic westerns of its own, often with Hans Albers starring, adopted the methods of the first American westerns, and brought the Mexicans back as the stock villains. All of them were swarthy, had long mous-

taches, bristled with guns, and shouted "*Caramba!*" as the lead-in to every sentence, otherwise spoken in German. Either Mexicans didn't see these films, or felt it diplomatic to say nothing. But their hurt pride never fully healed.

In the 1950's, Warner Brothers made a series of wonderfully fast and savage cartoons, full of brilliant sight gags, in which the protagonists—villains and heroes alike—were all Mexicans. Mexican mice, cats, grasshoppers, crows. What offended the Mexicans this time was not that they were likened to mice

or insects, but that those creatures were invariably lazy, pictured as sleeping beneath huge sombreros in hammocks, sipping an occasional tequila, and generally engaging in a non-stop siesta. Once more there were official government protests, but this time they were only academic, since the series in question had run its course anyway before any action could be taken.

Through the years, Hollywood frequently had trouble with minority representatives who felt that their race had been slighted when a movie had an Armenian seducer or a Dutch murderer. Usually, the

Frank Lackteen, a serial witch doctor from time immemorial, is about to sacrifice Frances Gifford to the current gods in *Jungle Girl* (1940).

64

Since the Devil obviously cannot be American, presumably he also must fall under the heading of "foreign" villains. Of the many actors to play the supreme villain of them all, none was more successful than Walter Huston, who played him with both menace and rascally humor in *The Devil and Daniel Webster* (1941), with Edward Arnold as Webster.

minor tempests in a teapot were adroitly side-stepped, since no one race was being systematically maligned. And if a Dutchman or a Frenchman thought his country was being vilified, the rejoinder was always to look at *Rembrandt* or *Louis Pasteur* in which the same country was thoroughly glorified through one of her native sons.

But the gangster era of the late 1920's and early 1930's was something else again. Regardless of Enrico Caruso, Rudolph Valentino, and Mayor LaGuardia, regardless of the thousands of honest and gainfully em-

ployed Italians in the United States, Al Capone and his gangster cohorts did seem to be of predominantly Italian heritage. And, with the news—and the names—screaming from newspaper headlines every day—what reason to back away from the truth by making them British or French or American. So, with pronounced Italian accents, and greasy hair, Paul Muni, Edward G. Robinson, George Raft, Osgood Perkins, and others became movie Italians. Perhaps all would have been well if they hadn't developed stereotyped traits that probably offended the law-abiding Italians as much as

Monte Blue, center, as the diabolical ruler of Atlantis in *Undersea Kingdom* (1936).

Greatest "Outer Space" villain of all was Ming, Emperor of Mongo, who opposed Buster Crabbe in three Flash Gordon serials. Ming was played by Charles Middleton, also an expert shyster lawyer and, because of his mean face, truant officer!

After Monte Blue and Charles Middleton, Gene Stutenroth made a rather rundown and cheaply garbed interplanetary ruler in *Captain Video* in the fifties.

their criminal careers. Most of them were basically illiterates, speaking in broken English, and using their ill-gotten wealth to "buy" culture in the form of expensive furnishings, paintings, etc. And most of them showed a predilection for high-toned mistresses, all of them American, and, if possible, from high society. As one gang-lord took over another's territory, he took over his woman too!

The movies answered the protests rather feebly. *Scarface*, for example, the best of all the gangster epics, but literally infested with Italians, had a discussion in a newspaper office in which honest Italians protested the shame that a few were bringing on the many. And Scarface himself was finally brought to justice by an honest Italian cop, played by C. Henry Gordon. When gangsterism came back to the movies in the 1950's, the Italian protests were anticipated in advance, and the scripts of *Al Capone* and the Mafia story, *Pay or Die* (built around a heroic Italian policeman), headed off most of the objections.

Since the cold war, of course, it is the Russians who have been most frequently cast in villainous molds. They are hardly in a position to protest, or to have much attention paid to their protests if they did, so, replacing the Mexicans and the Italians, they are liable to be around for a long time as our most convenient villains if we *must* have a foreign bad guy, and don't want to risk offending the Samoans or the Outer Mongolians.

# THE GANGSTERS
## AND THE HOODS

Edward G. Robinson in *Little Caesar* (1931).

The gangster cycle in movies is rightly placed at the end of the 1920's and the beginning of the 1930's—the climactic years of the Prohibition era. Yet, it is astonishing that, as with the western, the roots of the gangster film go back to the movies' infancy. The first important gangster film, D. W. Griffith's *Musketeers of Pig Alley*, made in New York in 1912, already included in its tight one-reel of footage such soon-to-be standard ingredients as the innocent hero and heroine unwittingly embroiled between rival gangster factions. Here, it was Lillian Gish and Walter Miller; almost thirty years later, in *The Roaring 20's*, Priscilla Lane and Jeffrey Lynn were to enact identical roles. The film also established the saloon and the dance-hall as standard gangster backdrops, acknowledged that the "smart" crook got away with it by paying off the cops, and even introduced in Elmer Booth (an excel-lent actor who died before his career was really under way) an incredibly prophetic forerunner of the Cagney gangster, complete with the nervous hand movements, quick grin, and facial mannerisms that were to become Cagney characteristics. To Booth, a little-known and now forgotten actor, must go the credit for being the first individual and three-dimensional screen gangster. Other gangster movies of the 1912 to 1916 years, such as Ince's *The Gangsters and the Girl* and Selig's *The Making of Crooks* introduced such additional themes as the cop masquerading as a crook in order to round up the gang, and the pool hall as a breeding ground of crime and a nurturer of juvenile delinquency.

But the gangster film as a genre only began to come into its own in the mid- and late-1920's, via such films as *A City Gone Wild*, *Underworld*, and *The*

Cagney and Robinson in their only film together: *Smart Money* (1931).

Robinson in typical pose, giving orders to Joe Sawyer.

Robinson in a dual role in *The Whole Town's Talking*, an exciting—and amusing—semi-lampoon of gangster movies made by John Ford in 1934.

Three generations of tough guys join forces: Robinson from the thirties, Alan Ladd from the forties, Paul Stewart from the fifties—in *Hell on Frisco Bay* (1955).

Racket. The movies however, were hard pressed to match the violence, crime, and viciousness that screamed at the public from newspaper headlines—and, in order to try to do so, the movie gangster became an unsubtle, superficial stereotype, an uncouth thug operating by brute strength alone, and more often than not played by Fred Kohler. There was an interesting break from tradition, however, in 1929's *Walking Back*, in which two dapper and cultured gangsters—played by Ivan Lebedeff and George E. Stone—indulge in some prolonged staccato dialogue (via titles) so akin to that used by the paid assassins in "The Killers" (complete even to the repeated and sar-

James Cagney and Mae Clarke in *The Public Enemy* (1931).

Cagney and pal Eddie Woods try to pick up Jean Harlow in *The Public Enemy* (1931).

Cagney and his "boys" in traditional gangster stance, before a showdown.

70

Cagney and George Raft in stir again: *Each Dawn I Die* (1939).

A typical Cagney finish: gunned down on the steps of a church. With Gladys George and Charles Wilson in *The Roaring 20's* (1939).

THE MANAGEMENT WILL NOT TOLERATE ROUGH STUFF OR FIGHTING IN THIS DRESSING ROOM.

NO SMOKING

A later but no less dynamic Cagney in the excellent biography of Ruth Etting, *Love Me or Leave Me* (1955), with Doris Day as the singer who becomes involved with a gangster.

71

Humphrey Bogart: last of the "Big 3" movie gangsters to appear and seemingly the least of them, Bogart went on to become the biggest star of them all. Less mannered than his two predecessors, and with a wry sense of humor, Bogie, whether bad guy or good, was the movies' foremost "tough guy"—and lived up to his reputation off-screen too!

castic use of the phrase "Bright boy") that one can't help but wonder whether Ernest Hemingway hadn't seen that little-known picture, and enlarged on those two characters when he wrote "The Killers."

With the coming of sound, the gangster film began to flourish as never before, and a change of emphasis in the mid-1930's—the limelight now centered on the law-*enforcer* rather than on the law-*breaker*—made no essential changes in the type-casting that had evolved. For the most part, the social status of the gangster was a rigidly adhered-to affair, and Hollywood mobsters were shunted into one of three basic categories. First, there were the "elite" gang bosses—those happy few who combined brains, brawn, courage, and initiative. Second, there was a smaller and rarely seen group that might be characterized as the "higher-ups"—the bosses of the bosses, the crooked politicians, the men who carefully broke no laws themselves, yet profited by the crimes of others, the "Mr. Big's" who were above the law and quite often didn't even get caught. The third and largest category of course consists of the hired help—the hoods, goons, and gunmen who themselves could be broken up into individual groupings.

Of the gang bosses, there can be no doubt that Edward G. Robinson, dynamic and single-purposed; James Cagney, jaunty, chip-on-his-shoulder, possessed of a sense of humor even at his most murderous, and generally the most sympathetic of the trio; and Humphrey Bogart, callous, cynical, entirely cold-blooded, were the king-pins. Lew Ayres (*Doorway to Hell*) and Paul Muni (*Scarface*) were transient but impressive candidates for membership in the club, as was Clark Gable, who in 1931 and 1932 was roughing 'em up at MGM as a ruthless, charming, lady-slapping heel much as Cagney was doing over at Warner's. John

The grim, rather talkative *The Petrified Forest* (1936), in which Bogart's vicious Duke Mantee quite stole the limelight from Robert E. Sherwood's stylish prose, and from official stars Leslie Howard and Bette Davis.

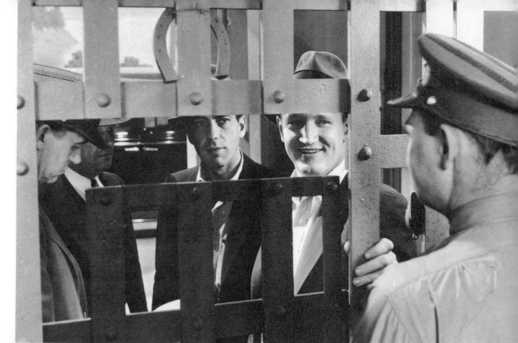

Bogart and Joseph Sawyer arrive at the Big House in *San Quentin* (1937).

Bogart squelches stoolie Ernie Adams in *San Quentin* (1937).

Humphrey Bogart with Joel Mc-Crea, Allen Jenkins and Charles Halton in 1937's *Dead End*, which served to boost Bogie's criminal career.

Bogart, Cagney and Jeffrey Lynn
in another crackling prohibition-
era saga. From Warner's *The Roaring 20's.*

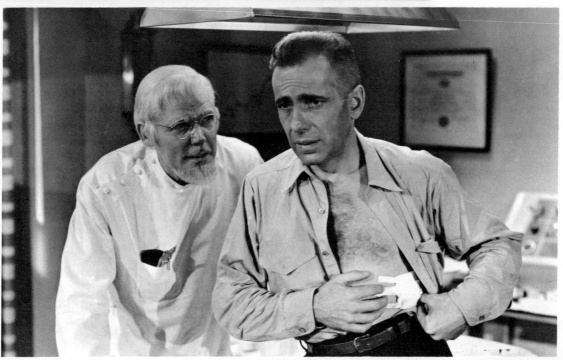

Directed by Raoul Walsh and written by John Huston, *High Sierra*
(1941) was one of Bogart's best and
most literate gangster films; with
Henry Hull.

The screen's first gangster film: Lillian Gish, a Cagneyish Elmer Booth and Harry Carey in *The Musketeers of Pig Alley* (1912).

Gilbert even had a tentative stab at polished gangsterism in this period. Runners-up to the Robinson-Cagney-Bogart dynasty throughout the 1930's were such efficient if lesser gang bosses (usually conducting the gangster business in "B" or lesser "A" pictures) as Ricardo Cortez, Cy Kendall, Joseph Calleia, Lloyd Nolan, Cesar Romero, and Bruce Cabot. The latter three later switched to predominantly hero roles, Nolan scoring on his breezy self-assurance, Romero on his charm and sense of comedy, and Cabot on his rugged masculinity. But all seemed served best by villainy.

The "higher-ups" were, by the very nature of things, rarely seen—and then only briefly. They represented the omnipotence of power above the law; they had a culture and veneer (usually they were from the "best" families) that the self-made Robinson type of gangster could only admire and never dream of dupli-cating; and their unseen presence was used to cow those upstarts who were too ambitious, or wanted to move out of their allotted territory. This character in *Little Caesar* was known only as "The Big Boy," and was played expertly by that veteran smoothie, Sidney Blackmer. Plump, greasy Edwin Maxwell, a cigar forever clamped between his teeth, a sort of Sydney Greenstreet minus a sense of humor, was an excellent villain in any walk of life, but a particularly apt "Mr. Big." Hearty Ralph Ince (a good movie director also), fur-coated, attended by a legion of dress-suited bodyguards, was another "untouchable." So, to a lesser degree, was William Boyd, who, to avoid confusion with the better-known DeMille star of the same name (who later became Hopalong Cassidy), billed himself as William "Stage" Boyd.

In appropriate gangster tradition, few of the "hoods" ever really escaped their environment and

Dick Cramer at extreme left, old Fairbanksian villain Frank Campeau (in derby) and Ben Lyon in rather offbeat gang film from 1930, *Soldier's Plaything*.

Lon Chaney played a big city gangster as convincingly as he played freaks and monsters.

Corrupt newspaperman Richard Barthelmess and untouchable gang boss Clark Gable in 1931's *The Finger Points*, based on the murder of newspaper reporter Jake Lingle.

Another of several early Gable gangster roles: with John Mack Brown in *The Secret Six* (1931).

Spencer Tracy, too, was a gangster in several early talkies: in *20,000 Years in Sing Sing* he threatens Lyle Talbot, who was a favorite heavy in "A" movies and a good hero in "B" pictures.

overthrew their bosses. George Raft, who started out as an apprentice gunman and all-around henchman in *Scarface* and *Palmy Days* was an exception of sorts. By the late 1930's, in films like *Each Dawn I Die*, Raft was occasionally running his own mob, but a more romantic image was sought for him, and his criminal activity was sporadic. Boris Karloff was visually an ex-

cellent hood in *Scarface* and one or two other early gangster films, and a convincing rat in *Five Star Final* (where he was a divinity student discharged for sexual degeneracy!) but his well-modulated British accent seemed ill at ease in squabbles about who was to run the East Side, and he soon escaped to bigger and badder things.

George E. Stone goes through the dreaded "little green door" in *The Last Mile* (1932).

Vince Barnett, Osgood Perkins, George Raft, and Paul Muni in *Scarface* (1932).

But, for the rest, it was once a hood, always a hood, although occasionally the small-time punks were allowed to vary their professions a little. There was no meaner, more vicious, trigger-happy gunman than Barton MacLane, who never spoke when shouting would do. Joe Sawyer, J. Carrol Naish, Ward Bond, Anthony Quinn, Marc Lawrence, Ed Pawley, Noel Madison, Jack LaRue, and Paul Guilfoyle were pillars of strength in many a kidnapping or bank-robbing heist. Small of stature and possessed of usefully weak chins and shifty eyes, Paul Fix and Ernie Adams were the perennial finks and squealers who invariably "got theirs" in the boiler rooms of San Quentin, or while cowering in a corner of a poolroom. And, of course, the gangster royalty had to have its court jesters—principally in the forms of diminutive Vince Barnett; pop-eyed and rather lovable Edward Brophy; and in the dumb tough guys of Warren Hymer and Stanley Fields, always willing to do the boss's dirty work, and somehow always muffing it. Fields did occasionally play a gang-

The slimiest of wardheelers, Edwin Maxwell, has his bribe pushed aside by an honest James Cagney in *G Men* (1935).

Ed Brophy, Warren Hymer, Bruce Cabot and Cesar Romero make a formidable quartet in *Show Them No Mercy* (1935).

ster straight—but the image of stupidity was too firmly implanted for audiences ever to take him too seriously.

From the 1940's on, the vintage gangster film became increasingly rare. Cagney in *The Roaring 20's* and *White Heat*, Bogart in *High Sierra* and *The Big Shot*, and Robinson in *Key Largo* and *Hell on Frisco Bay* kept the old flag flying at increasingly rare intervals. From a dozen different directions, the water was being muddied. Former romantic stars such as Robert Montgomery and Robert Taylor entered the

gangster arena, begging for a kind of "understanding" that Bogart or Robinson would have scorned. The detective novels of Dashiell Hammett and Raymond Chandler were enjoying a new popularity, and lawlessness on the screen became more of a matter of intricately plotted murders and webs of counter-plots than the simple organization of nationwide crime. A new breed of leading-man—Kirk Douglas, Burt Lancaster, Richard Widmark, Jack Palance, Steve Cochrane, Lawrence Tierney—brought viciousness and

Larry "Buster" Crabbe and Anthony Quinn in *Tip-Off Girls* (1938).

Barton MacLane tries to break out
—again—in *Mutiny in the Big
House* (1938).

Big boss Sidney Blackmer, with
triggermen Carleton Young and
Norman Willis, in *Convict's Code*
(1939).

Alan Ladd's first big hit: *This
Gun for Hire* (1942).

Sadistic strong-arm man William Bendix and smoothie Joseph Calleia in *The Glass Key* (1942).

A well-lit atmospheric setup from *The Gangster* (1947): John Kellog, Sheldon Leonard, Akim Tamiroff and Barry Sullivan.

Kirk Douglas came to the fore as a slick modern gangster, using corporation chicanery rather than strong-arm crime, in 1947's *I Walk Alone* with Lizabeth Scott.

Charles McGraw, one of "the Killers" in the film of that name, was one of the more interesting new gangster villains of the forties. With Virginia Grey in *The Threat* (1949).

Though he has played as many good guys as bad, Stephen McNally has always been most effective on the wrong side of the law. As the killer in *Woman in Hiding* (1949), with Peggy Dow as the mistress he eventually murders.

*The Night and the City* (1950): Richard Widmark, Mike Mazurki.

*The Mob* (1951): Neville Brand and Broderick Crawford.

*He Ran All the Way* (1951): John Garfield's last film, with Shelley Winters, Wallace Ford.

*The Long Wait* (1953): the Spillane collision of sex and violence —with Peggie Castle, Anthony Quinn, William Conrad.

*The Asphalt Jungle* (1954): a classic among crime films. With Sterling Hayden, Anthony Caruso, Sam Jaffe.

Rod Steiger as Al Capone (1959).

*The Asphalt Jungle*: Marc Lawrence, Sam Jaffe.

Kane Richmond

Byron Foulger

Gene Lockhart

Jack LaRue

Paul Guilfoyle

Lawrence Tierney

Eduardo Cianelli

Lloyd Nolan

J. Carroll Naish

Mathew Betz        Ricardo Cortez        Robert Blake

rugged or off-beat good-looks to criminal careers that were motivated by complexes rather than sheer honest greed. All of these players attained their considerable popularity via badman roles, and then promptly reformed—with decidedly less interesting results.

As for the rest of the overlords of crime, the literary source material of so many of the new movie thrillers overloaded us with that delightful but overfamiliar cliché figure, the suave master-criminal who *hates* violence. It might be added, however, that such "polite" villains as Howard da Silva, Luther Adler, Thomas Gomez, Sydney Greenstreet, Morris Carnovsky, and Walter Slezak invariably had a full coterie of half-witted psychotic strong-arm men (Mike Mazurki, William Bendix, Neville Brand, Harry Landers) who, between giggles, were delighted to beat Alan Ladd and Edmond O'Brien to a bloody pulp.

In the 1960's, the gangster tradition seemed to acquire a new vigor, but without discipline. There was a prolific but undistinguished attempt at a new cycle of "vintage" gangster films—*Al Capone, The Rise and Fall of Legs Diamond, Baby-Face Nelson*—all of which fell short of the classics of yesteryear, either because of cheapness of budget, carelessness in recreating the essential period atmosphere, or inadequate casting that had "method" and "motivation" actors floundering about in a self-created morass that must have pained such dynamic old maestros as Robinson and Cagney. Contemporary gangster films have been few, the best perhaps being Fritz Lang's *The Big Heat* of 1953, and, to a much lesser but still interesting degree, Joseph Lewis' *The Big Combo* of 1955. Both of these stressed the "combine" machinery and efficiency of modern crime, and the law's biggest problem—not of *catching* the criminal—but of *proving* that he is a criminal.

The days of Joe Sawyer and Barton MacLane storming into the First National Bank with tommy guns are over. While it's probably a good deal safer for the innocent passer-by in the street, it's also a good deal less fun for the moviegoer!

# THE BEDROOM
## VILLAINS

Sessue Hayakawa and Fannie Ward in *The Cheat* (1915).

Few aspects of movie villainy have changed as much over the years as the eternal problem of luring the innocent heroine into the nearest bedroom. That word "innocent" is important, since the lechers and would-be seducers of the movies, invariably surrounded on all sides by beautiful and willing damsels, have nevertheless gone to extraordinary lengths to get the virtuous (and usually somewhat dull) heroine into their power. Early heroines, frequently both ultra-virtuous and ultra-helpless in the best Victorian tradition, were not even supposed to know about sex, and thus their frantically energetic efforts to escape the fate reputedly worse than death were not always entirely logical.

In those charmingly unsophisticated years before 1920—the years of heroines like Mary Pickford and Mary Miles Minter, and equally virtuous heroes like Doug Fairbanks and Charles Ray—sex reared its ugly head occasionally, but never too drastically or explicitly. The frankness of Cecil B. DeMille's 1915 *The Cheat*, a classic sex yarn remade several times, was distinctly unusual for the period. A society woman (Fanny Ward), desperately in need of money, borrows it from a Burmese merchant (Sessue Hayakawa) and agrees to surrender herself to him if she cannot repay the loan by a certain time. She is confident of course both of being able to repay, and of talking the gentlemanly Burmese out of the bargain if worse comes to worst. It does, and he turns out to be no gentleman at all. When she resists his violent advances, he brands her on the back with the same mark that he burns onto all his "possessions." For perhaps the first time, the bedroom villain emerged as a *real* and frightening menace, and not just as the stock figure who precipitated the suspense and climactic chase. However, *The Cheat* stacked the cards a little. The dubious morals of a woman who would make such a bargain to begin with, and then compound her misdeeds by reneging, were all swept aside by the fact that the other man was a *Burmese*. It thus became a racial rather than a moral issue, with audience sympathy directed solely at the rather heartless heroine rather than at the sorely-tried villain who after all *had* fulfilled his part of the bargain quite honorably. It is significant, too, that the rape itself was prevented. Successful rape and/or seduction was rare in the pre-1920 years because of the prevailing Victorian moral code. Audiences, it was felt, just wouldn't accept a heroine who they had seen so treated, even if she was entirely blameless. Thus, in the novel *The Clansman*, the heroine and her mother are raped, and *then* commit suicide by jumping off a cliff to end "the shame that neither they nor the world could forget." In *The Birth of a Nation* (the 1915 film version of that inflammatory novel), however, the girl (Mae Marsh) kills herself by jumping off the cliff to *avoid* rape, and her death-scene is followed by the title "For she who had learned the stern lesson of honor, we should not grieve that she found far sweeter the gates of death."

The first real sign of change took place in 1920, interestingly enough in two Griffith films. In *The Greatest Question*, Lillian Gish played a typically naive and helpless heroine, an orphan, who finds herself working for a singularly lustful old man, played by George Nicholls. The titles frequently tell us that he has "lascivious eyes" and "base passions," yet, despite all sorts of hints, poor Lillian never gets the message until the end of the sixth reel, when, tired of subtler approaches, Nicholls locks the door behind them and tries brute strength. (It is incredible how much physical agility young virgins seem to show in fighting off hulking attackers three times their weight and size!) But, even then, innocence prevails. Rescued by boy friend Bobby Harron, she embraces him for the fadeout, but both agree, "We don't know enough to get married yet." This kind of innocence was superbly parodied by Will Rogers in one of his two-reel comedies of the period called *Uncensored Movies*. As the heroine is carried off by the lustful villain, Rogers rallies a group of listless farmers with the title "Are you going to sit there shootin' craps while an American woman is carried off?" The heroine fights the villain for her honor, and finally Rogers breaks down the door of the villain's cabin. "Let me look into your eyes," he asks the girl sternly, and then, with a sigh of relief, "Thank heavens, I'm in time!"

But, to revert to Griffith and Lillian Gish. In *Way Down East*, also of 1920, she plays another innocent, but also—for the first time—a mature and sensitive woman. Swept off her feet by a dashing city playboy, she is tricked into a mock marriage, from which an illegitimate child results. Although she is blameless, she is of course ostracized. Griffith used the film to condemn puritanical bigots—but he was also realistic enough not to be too harsh with the philandering playboy. What earlier had been a cardinal crime was now accepted as a moral one only, and the playboy goes unpunished to continue his philandering with other victims. As the seducer, Lennox Sanderson, Lowell Sherman was superb, and the first great boudoir villain of the movies. He was handsome and per-suasive, so his success with the ladies was easy to understand. He underplayed, using only a gesture or two—a gasp of anticipation, or a clenching of the fists in nervous excitement—to express the sexual excitement so important to the character. And he was human enough to have moments of doubt and remorse. His Lennox Sanderson was the blueprint for most of the subsequent bedroom villains, although far too many of them lacked his polish, and painted their characters in the deepest dyes of black. The role remained a Sherman specialty, although, as the movies grew more sophisticated, his approach was less serious. In 1928's *The Garden of Eden*, a charming and witty comedy in the Lubitsch tradition, his philanderer was an amiable spoof of Lennox Sanderson, selecting his girls with a debonair flourish from a "menu" listing such items as "fresh young squab." Sherman was the peer of his class in the sound era too, playing the same kind of role in *The Greeks Had a Word for Them*, which he directed with the same elegance that he gave to his acting.

*Way Down East*, then, brought the sophisticated man-about-town seducer into prominence—but the heroine was still virtuous. It still took a wedding, even if a phoney one, to "justify" her seduction to the audience. But the next year, there was another change. The war had been over for three years now. The 1920's were under way. It was a restless period and audiences wanted new "kicks," new sophistication, new faces—and less of the old values, including "innocence." Rudolph Valentino, previously typed as an *unsympathetic* gigolo because of his unfashionable Latin looks, became a star overnight when his torrid—and unconventional—lovemaking suddenly seemed to

Over twenty years later, Sessue had similar designs on the virtue of Mireille Balin in *L'Enfer du Jeu* (1939).

Lowell Sherman, the master bedroom diplomat, with Lillian Gish in *Way Down East* (1920).

know?"—indicated that movie heroines were growing up, and *did* know about sex! As in *The Cheat*, their love story had something of the forbidden fruit angle in that the heroine was a white girl, and he an Arab. But, of course, this was tidily cleared up in the final reel with the neat explanation that he was really a titled Englishman who had merely been brought up in the desert.

Hot on the heels of *The Sheik* came Erich von Stroheim's *Foolish Wives*, in which a sexually degenerate Russian officer was the *central* character in a story that had no hero at all. From then on, the movie heroine's intrinsic innocence was a thing of the past. In *Son of the Sheik* (1926), Valentino rapes the heroine (Vilma Banky)—and the situation is accepted. In *The Scarlet Letter*, Lillian Gish has an adulterous affair with a minister (Lars Hanson), and a child results. Again, the situation is accepted maturely, without "compensating" factors or last-minute tidying-up. The success of more mature and realistic treatments of love and sex in films from Europe not only made Hollywood stars out of European players (Garbo, Pola Negri, Lya de Putti) but resulted in directors like Ernst Lubitsch coming over too, to add their sophistication to the Hollywood product, and to be copied by Hollywood directors.

With sex being treated far more freely (and usually with good taste) on the screen in both comedies and dramas, the 1920's became a spawning ground for a whole new crop of bedroom villains, none of whom quite matched Lowell Sherman, but many of whom were quite unique. As remarkable in his own way as Sherman, but at the other end of the scale, was Roy D'Arcy, who played the robustly lecherous villain in the Erich von Stroheim-directed *The Merry Widow*. Seemingly resentful of the fact that he had

fill the bill for something new and daring. Agnes Ayres, the heroine of his 1921 *The Sheik*, is abducted by the desert chieftain, and asks him, "Why have you brought me here?"

His reply—"Are you not woman enough to

Erich von Stroheim and the cryptically billed Miss Dupont in *Foolish Wives* (1922).

Roy D'Arcy's leer failed to triumph over John Gilbert's smile for the affections of Mae Murray in *The Merry Widow* (1931).

not been allowed to play the role himself, von Stroheim gave D'Arcy his head, and the result was the most outrageous piece of ham—bar none—ever seen on the American screen. Immaculately dressed in spotless white uniforms, D'Arcy clicked his heels, saluted, bowed, adjusted his monocle, flashed his eyes, and leered—and leered—and leered, revealing a set of white teeth that sparkled and gleamed as they reflected light from the dazzling decor, and from the arc lights themselves. D'Arcy never lived down that amazing performance, and was only called on after that by directors who needed bravura villainy. He attempted to repeat his seductive pyrotechnics in *La Bohème* the following year, but director King Vidor and star Lillian Gish managed to keep him more successfully under control. The gleaming sneer of a smile was still there, and so was the mincing walk, but the role was less dominant and with (presumably) many of his more exuberant outbursts left on the cutting room floor, D'Arcy managed somehow to fit into the more sombre framework of *La Bohème*.

Von Stroheim, of course, was seldom satisfied with just *one* villain, and sharing D'Arcy's bedroom escapades in *The Merry Widow* was the less dashing but infinitely better actor, Tully Marshall. A veteran character actor, but never better than as a cunning, crotchety, and usually lascivious villain (as also in the much later *This Gun for Hire*), Marshall had one of the roles of his career in *The Merry Widow* as the degenerate Baron Sadoja, a crippled foot-fetishist who likes to conduct his amours in beds covered by black silk sheets, and who finally dies of a heart attack caused by the excitement of his wedding night!

On a more civilized and polished level, Adolphe Menjou and, to a lesser degree, William Powell became suave exponents of the boudoir seduction—both as villains and as more sympathetic roués. Ivan Lebedeff tried literally to follow in Valentino's footsteps by replaying one of the Latin lover's gigolo roles in *The Loves of Sunya*, a Gloria Swanson vehicle that was a remake of Clara Kimball Young's *The Eyes of Youth*. Framing Gloria in a compromising situation, Lebedeff attacked her in his bedroom just as her husband and several witnesses, seeking evidence for a divorce, broke in. Lebedeff made an admirably despicable villain, but, despite his good looks, he was never able to emulate Valentino by graduating from gigolos to romantic leads.

The impact of the bedroom villain lessened a trifle in the early talkies. In the realistic, dog-eat-dog dramas and comedies that were so much a part of the Depression years, the girl forced to spend a night with a man she didn't love—or in some cases, *did* love—soon came to be accepted quite casually as one of the facts of life. Audiences could hardly be expected to be aghast at villains for doing exactly what such heroes as Spencer Tracy, Ben Lyon, Donald Cook, Richard Barthelmess, James Cagney, and Frederic March were doing. And, with the big "moral clean-up" of 1934, when the industry's self-imposed housecleaning and censorship took a lot of the guts—and fun—out of moviegoing, the boudoir heavy found himself restricted more than ever.

The mid-1930's in Hollywood were aimed at the great American family. Mae West was supplanted by Shirley Temple and Deanna Durbin, and the movies were once more back in that pre-1920 age of innocence when actual rape and seduction were rare, and when the *threat* of it (rather than the consequences of it) was what caused all the excitement. Once again, it was

Fuller Mellish Jr. as the seedy burlesque performer who lives with,
and off, the star, Helen Morgan, in
Rouben Mamoulian's brilliant first
film, *Applause* (1929).

fashionable for the heroines to be appetizingly virginal, this reaching a kind of self-parody in the Dorothy Lamour South Sea island romantic adventures. Invariably, Dorothy would be pursued by a native chieftain with distinctly Park Avenue bedroom ideas (poor J. Carrol Naish was one of the chief malefactors, invariably being eaten by crocodiles or swamped in a typhoon before he'd gotten very far with the White Goddess) and equally invariably she would meet her first white man (Ray Milland, Jon Hall) who would explain to her what a kiss was!

Just as the end of World War One brought about the demise of the first era of innocence, so was the Never-Never-Land of the 1930's brought to its close by the advent of World War Two. But audiences that had been through the Depression and were now going through a war just couldn't be convinced of the overpowering importance of innocence, or of the unspeakable evil of seduction. The bedroom villains of yore never regained their pre-eminence, and indeed there seemed to be a tendency to whitewash them and turn them into heroes. Throughout the 1940's and 1950's, Melvyn Douglas, Gary Cooper, Cary Grant, and Clark Gable found themselves more and more playing astute bedroom diplomats who are finally trapped into marriage when they run across the *one* girl who insists on a wedding before bedding.

Since the late 1950's, and the success of films such as *Room at the Top* and, in a lighter vein, *Love with the Proper Stranger*, the moral decline of the hero—who cheats, swears, sleeps around, and generally does everything that the former villains did with far more

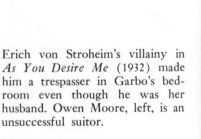

Erich von Stroheim's villainy in
*As You Desire Me* (1932) made
him a trespasser in Garbo's bedroom even though he was her
husband. Owen Moore, left, is an
unsuccessful suitor.

92

Marital morals muddied the waters somewhat in the early sound era. In 1931, James Rennie was a good guy who made love to Barbara Stanwyck in *Illicit* and Monroe Owsley a bad guy who made love to Claudette Colbert in *Honor Among Lovers*, but there was little basic difference in their screen characters.

charm and savoir-faire—has been such that the Lowell Sherman brand of lechery doesn't stand a chance any more. For not only does the new "hero" ill-use his women, but he does so without grace or gratitude, as though such were his right in the modern world against which he is so inexplicably in rebellion. By comparison, Lennox Sanderson in *Way Down East* was a prince among men. If nothing else, the old-time seducer was invariably a gentleman who played his women as an angler plays the fish on his line, trying persuasion, coercion, and consummate trickery to achieve his end. Today's "hero," on the other hand, is almost never a gentleman, and takes his women without wasting *any* time on finesse. And since the "heroines" aren't particularly ladylike either, the threat to their honor—if it still remains—has ceased to be of paramount importance. Indeed, by the early 1960's, the only sustained innocence left on the American screen reposed in the improbably mature virgins played by Doris Day, and the new, "modern" bedroom villains had changed into the aggressive *females* seeking out the younger innocent males as *their* prey!

THE

# MONSTERS

The movies' first Frankenstein monster—from Edison's one-reel version of the horror classic in 1910.

Today's youngsters, used to taking Frankenstein and Dracula for granted through seeing them in theaters, at their own kiddie matinees, and on television, must look on their parents with a condescending pity. For while the silents had just about everything else, they didn't have a well-established tradition of horror films —and movie monsters were rare. To be sure, there was always the occasional science-fiction thriller (like *The Wizard*) with its ape-man, or the serials (Houdini's *The Master Mystery* being a good example) with their terrifying robots. But vampires, werewolves, "things" from outer space, and laboratory-constructed monsters were conspicuous by their almost total absence. And yet, most of the monsters that became such old friends—and such boxoffice winners—in the sound era had at least one or two forerunners in the early years.

*Frankenstein* was brought to the screen at least twice prior to 1915, once by the Thomas Edison Studios. Stills indicate that the monster was quite fearsome, and that the laboratory scenes were well-staged and convincing. Another early essay into this kind of horror was provided by *Murders in the Rue Morgue*.

But it was in Germany, in the early 1920's, that the screen's first clear-cut horror cycle came into be-

Boris Karloff as the Monster in *Frankenstein* (1931).

96

Dwight Frye, dwarf, insane laboratory assistant and general hanger-on in the Frankenstein films, taunts the Monster with the only thing it really fears—fire—in *Frankenstein*.

ing—although the films were planned primarily as fantasies, drawing heavily on Germanic legends, and offering psychological content as well as Grand Guignol material. Scaring the audience was *not* the initial intent of these films, although by their mystic terror, grim, foreboding sets and frequent savagery of action, they most certainly qualify in the horror category.

*The Cabinet of Dr. Caligari* was the first, with Conrad Veidt as the terrifying somnambulist murderer. *The Golem*, which followed, presented Paul Wegener as the legendary man of stone who is brought to life by black magic to bring about retribution for the oppression heaped on his people. Many of the German fantasies of this period today seem like interesting

In his third time round as the Monster in *Son of Frankenstein* (1939) Karloff found a loyal friend in the mad shepherd Ygor (Bela Lugosi), whose broken neck is the result of once having been hanged!

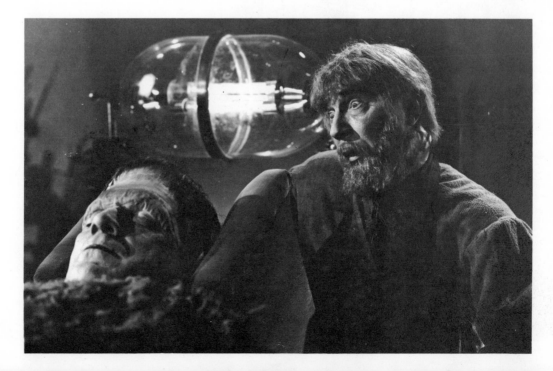

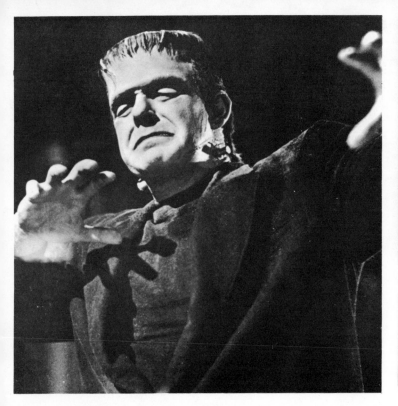

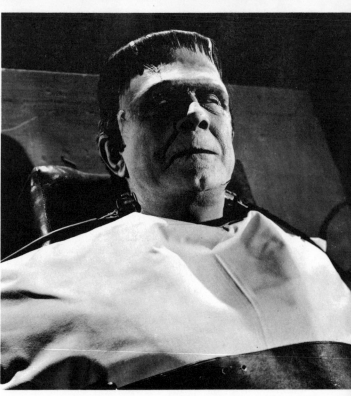

In *The Ghost of Frankenstein* (1942) Lon Chaney Jr. took over as the Monster.

*Frankenstein Meets the Wolf Man* (1943) introduced Bela Lugosi to the role of the Monster.

Chaney battles Lugosi in the climactic sequence of *Frankenstein Meets the Wolf Man.*

landmarks, but do not stand up well in terms either of technique, dramatic content, or acting. *The Golem*, with its fast-pace, magnificent sets, and powerful performance from Wegener, does, however, stand up, and stand up well. In this film, one sees the source of many of the story ideas and individual incidents that were later to turn up so frequently in American horror films. The monster, for example, for all of his inhumanity and fearsome brute strength, has human qualities. He is lonely, and finds a temporary friend in a child too innocent to fear him. Boris Karloff's 1931 *Frankenstein* owes a great deal to this film of a decade earlier.

In 1922, Germany also produced the first vampire thriller with *Nosferatu*, a changed and romanticized but still recognizable version of *Dracula*. In many ways, it is still the most terrifying of all the Dracula films. Not only was Max Schreck's ghastly make-up as Dracula constantly changed, so that he seemed to

The first Dracula: Max Schreck in 1922's *Nosferatu*. Rumors persist that there was actually no such actor as Schreck (the name means "terror") and that it was just a pseudonym for the well-known German actor Alfred Abel.

Lon Chaney as the apparent vampire in 1927's *London After Midnight*; remade in the talkies as *Mark of the Vampire*.

The most famous vampire of all—
Bela Lugosi as Dracula (1931).

Bela Lugosi: *Dracula.*

Bela Lugosi, Helen Chandler,
Dwight Frye: *Dracula.*

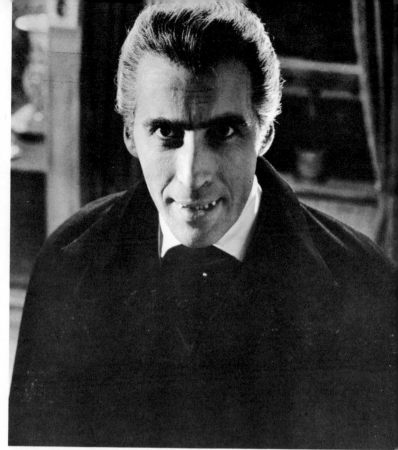

Christopher Lee in *The Horror of Dracula* (1958).

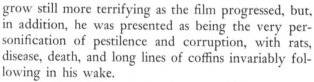

Lon Chaney Jr. and Louise Allbritton in *Son of Dracula* (1943).

Sex began to play an increasingly dominant part in the new vampire thrillers: *The Horror of Dracula*.

grow still more terrifying as the film progressed, but, in addition, he was presented as being the very personification of pestilence and corruption, with rats, disease, death, and long lines of coffins invariably following in his wake.

The list of German fantasy-horror films is an impressive one, but the films began to peter out in the mid-1920's, and it was Hollywood that took over the slowly formulating horror tradition. But the monsters were slow in coming. The "old house" thriller, depending so much on atmosphere, was admirably suited to the pictorial style of the silent screen, and it was this kind of horror film that dominated. *The Lost World* used brilliant special effects to bring prehistoric monsters to convincing life, and, in its over-all plot and treatment, it was a fascinating blueprint for the later *King Kong*, but it had no central monster-villain like Kong himself on whom to center attention.

The fine actor and brilliant pantomimist Lon Chaney made a whole series of thrillers and melodramas in the 1920's in which he played deformed or grotesque characters. Like Boris Karloff a decade later, he was able to command audience sympathy abso-

*Kiss of the Vampire* (1963) had a whole colony of vampires—and more emphasis on sex.

lutely no matter what shocking depredations his screen character was up to. In its physical impact, his Phantom of the Opera was undoubtedly his most striking and monstrous creation—yet it would be unfair to Chaney, and to a notable film, to dismiss it casually as just a monster movie.

Unquestionably, however, it was Karloff's monster in *Frankenstein*, and Bela Lugosi's vampire in *Dracula*, both of 1931, that set the whole monster cycle in motion so stylishly and so profitably. Sound brought not just dialogue, but mood-inspiring musical scores, and sound effects (the weird laboratory machinery, the howling wind, the barely heard tread of footsteps) to enhance the already considerable horror-manufacturing arsenal of special photographic effects, make-up, etc. The early horror films were grim, terrifying, slowly paced, relying as much on suggestion as on outright statement, and devoid of the blood, gore, and nauseating shock effects that made the much later horror films so unpalatable. And the early monsters too, were basically sympathetic. There was very real poignancy in Karloff's Frankenstein monster—driven

Henry Hull as the scientist turned werewolf in 1935's *Werewolf of London*.

Werewolf battles werewolf; Henry Hull and Warner Oland in *Werewolf of London.*

to kill by instincts he doesn't understand and by the cruelty of others, unable to communicate feelings and emotions often tenderer than those of his human persecutors. Even the movie werewolves had this built-in audience sympathy, and only the vampire—a Satanic, wholly evil creature—was ever presented as neither wanting, nor warranting, any kind of understanding or sympathy.

But vampires and werewolves (and later, a few offshoots such as cat people) pretty much exhausted the list of usable supernatural monsters. There was a

brief touch of novelty with Karloff's classic *The Mummy*, a superb horror film of 1932, but again, after the initial film, there was nothing more to say on the subject—as a whole string of grade "B" mummy films with Lon Chaney Jr. proved. The Frankenstein monster sustained itself surprisingly well through its first three films (*Bride of Frankenstein* and *Son of Frankenstein* were the follow-ups), but then Karloff left the series and the regular follow-ups quickly became cheap and standardized, reaching the depths of indignity when the various monsters at the Universal Studios

Evelyn Ankers, target of most movie monsters in the forties—just as Fay Wray had been in the thirties—meets Lon Chaney Jr. in 1941's *The Wolf Man.*

Officially "killed," Lon Chaney comes back to life again in *Frankenstein Meets the Wolf Man* (1943) when ghouls rob his grave.

were first of all co-starred in uninspired shockers, and then given to Abbott and Costello for a satire of the genre (*Abbott and Costello Meet Frankenstein*) which was a surprisingly bright spoof, but a sad end to the once great monster tradition. (Actually, of course, it proved not to be the end at all—in the late 1950's, monsters came back into vogue again, and Frankenstein and Dracula were put to work regularly, although, as before, in steadily deteriorating films.)

There is, after all, a limit to the number of ways a monster can be created—or to the kind of life he can lead once he's off the operating table. The first three

Frankenstein films from Universal did nobly by the idea, but most of the other man-made monsters were decidedly anticlimactic and usually quite pointless. They were created from the dead, or *restored* to life after death; they resulted from laboratory mishaps (exposure to electricity, or gas, or a serum that went wrong); they were apes with human brains transplanted into their skulls, or humans with apes' brains transplanted into their skulls; and almost all of them went on a last-reel rampage, destroying the laboratory and turning on the scientist who created them.

King Kong, the giant ape, enigmatically both hu-

In 1961's *Curse of the Werewolf*, serving-girl is attacked by beast-like madman—and the result is a little werewolf who grows up to be Oliver Reed.

104

Egyptian mummy Karloff comes back to life when his tomb is defiled by archaeologist Bramwell Fletcher: *The Mummy*, 1932.

man and sympathetic, and also just about the most vicious of all the monsters, was such an individual kind of heavy, and possessed such a distinct personality that it didn't seem at first as though he would produce too many imitations—especially since the special-effects work involved was both complex and expensive. There was a *Son of Kong*, and then apparently no more. But this kind of monster was revived in the post-World War Two years when it was discovered that atomic blasts and testing had disturbed, unfrozen, or otherwise liberated an astonishing variety of prehistoric monsters who had apparently slumbered in a kind of suspended animation since the dawn of time. Hollywood, and later Japan, England, and Sweden

produced a positive rash of these creatures, all of them following the basic continuity of *King Kong*, and winding up with a pitched battle in the appropriate metropolis (New York, Washington, San Francisco, London, Tokyo) in which the poor beast, a million or so years behind the times, was unfairly defeated by electricity, bombs, flame-throwers, rockets, and other modern weapons with which he was unfamiliar. None of these monsters had quite the engaging personality of the original Kong, and none of the films matched that classic original, since most of the producers were too anxious and had their monster on screen right away starting to pile up the shocks. The subtlety and brilliant construction of *King Kong* (in which nary a

In his new life, Karloff also finds a reincarnation of his old love, and wants to rekindle the flame. Zita Johann is his princess, and Noble Johnson stirs the cauldron.

105

monster appeared for the first half of the film, yet in which suspense was maintained steadily until it reached a fever pitch of exhausting excitement in the closing reels) was completely jettisoned in these new thrillers. However, the monsters themselves, the best of them created by Willis O'Brien (Kong's mentor) and his associate, Ray Harryhausen, were often beautifully created.

Also in the wake of the atomic age, with the realization that interplanetary travel was becoming a distinct possibility, came the realization that other

A 1940 sequel, *The Mummy's Hand*, had former western star Tom Tyler playing the Mummy.

Mummies, it seems, have lecherous intentions hardly in keeping with their years. Tyler is more interested in luscious Peggy Moran than in High Priest George Zucco. The impressive set was left over from James Whale's *Green Hell*.

Lon Chaney Jr. played the Mummy in *The Mummy's Tomb*, *The Mummy's Ghost* and *The Mummy's Curse*, and stalked through all of them in search of a girl friend.

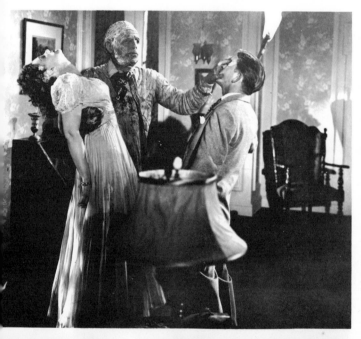

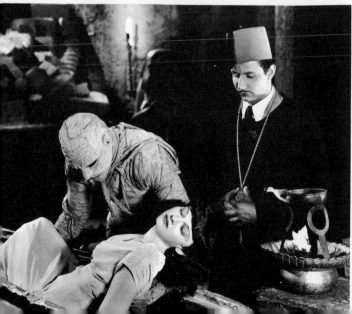

Paul Wegener as "the Golem" in the 1920 German classic of that title.

Lon Chaney Sr. in *The Phantom of the Opera* (1925).

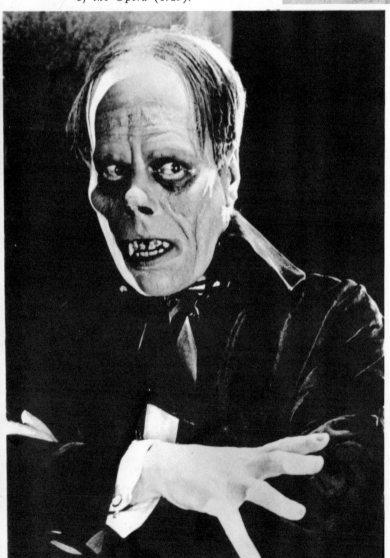

Chaney and Mary Philbin in *Phantom of the Opera*.

108

After Claude Rains had made a rather dignified Phantom in the forties, Herbert Lom played it for horror again in the third (1962) version.

Conrad Veidt in *The Man Who Laughs* (1928), an adaptation of the Victor Hugo tale about the man whose mouth had been carved into a permanent smile.

Another memorable Chaney characterization: as the "Hunchback of Notre Dame" (1923).

109

Conrad Veidt as the somnam-
bulist-killer Cesare, and Werner
Krauss as his evil mentor, in the
1919 *The Cabinet of Dr. Caligari.*

planets could produce monsters too—and that these could either invade earth en masse (as in one of the best of the science-fiction films, *War of the Worlds*) or arrive singly, as stowaways on rocket ships from earth that had made a successful round-trip. The bulk of these outer-space monsters were nightmares of modern art, human vegetables, "things" with giant eyes and long talons, and, in many cases, just huge blobs of self-enlarging jelly or slime. Earth-people tended to take them in their stride, and, when one of the first of them arrived in Universal's *It Came from Outer Space*, the townspeople knew exactly what to do. Grabbing the same lighted torches, the same extras (or their descendants) that had chased the Frankenstein mon-

ster through the countryside for the previous quarter of a century, now set out to destroy the one-eyed blob—which, like the Frankenstein monster, would probably have been quite harmless and even sociable if left alone!

Since the atom bomb fell, science itself—rather than the scientists—has become the villain, and it has been science that provoked the outer-space monsters, and has been responsible for the creation and unleashing of giant tarantulas, scorpions, ants, wasps, leeches, and sundry other variations of insect life. In the face of these, the man-made monsters, the vampires and the werewolves, have seemed rather tame, and it is perhaps to overcome this that producers have gone after shock

Wilfrid Walter was the blind half-
wit Jake in *Dark Eyes of London*,
1939 adaptation of an Edgar Wallace thriller. Greta Gynt is the
lady in the straitjacket.

110

Lon Chaney Jr. carries Anne Gwynne in the traditional
monster manner in 1941's *Man Made Monster*.

*King Kong* (1933)—still the monster-king of them all.

Scientist Charles Laughton reprimands the
ape-men he has created in *Island of Lost
Souls* (1932). Bela Lugosi is the ape-man in
the middle.

111

Exactly ten years later Lugosi was in the same kind of predicament in *The Ape Man*.

effects via detailed operation scenes, floating eyes, dismembered or decaying corpses, and a positive plethora of blood-letting. But our old monster friends of yore, like all old friends, are still the best. For all the shock effects of the later spine-chillers, the movies have never been able to top the unforgettable thrills of

Otto Kruger and ape-girl Vicky Lane in *Jungle Captive* (1945).

One of the more unique villains: an ambulatory (and amatory?) giant tree in *From Hell It Came* (1957).

King Kong battering down the gates, of the Frankenstein monster's first moments of life, Karloff's chillingly casual return to life when his tomb is defiled in *The Mummy*, or Lugosi's appreciative "Children of the night—what music they make!" as he listens to the howling of the wolves and guides his apprehensive guest through the crumbling cob-webbed ruins of Castle Dracula.

Rod Taylor and a Morlock in H. G. Wells's *The Time Machine* (1960).

# OTHER COUNTRIES'
## VILLAINS

The key word in this book is "Hollywood." When we refer to stars, directors, types of film, trends in villainy, audience reactions, we are referring primarily to those aspects of *American* film-making. Of course, there is a tremendous amount of internationalism in American cinema. Many of the crime films that had the biggest impact on American audiences were European imports. Directors such as Fritz Lang, Robert Siodmak, James Whale, and Alfred Hitchcock who made so many brilliant crime films, all came to Hollywood from Europe. Nor were Peter Lorre, Bela Lugosi, Boris Karloff, George Zucco, Basil Rathbone, and Erich von Stroheim Americans, although they made the bulk—and the best—of their films in this country.

All of the major movie-producing countries—and

Dean of all German villains: Rudolf Klein-Rogge, with Brigitte Helm in *Metropolis* (1926).

Fritz Rasp with Louise Brooks in *Diary of a Lost Girl* (1929).

Stig Jarrell (left) as the sadistic schoolmaster in the Swedish film *Torment* (1947), with Alf Kjellin.

Pedro Armendariz, right, seen with Gilbert Roland in *The Torch* (1950), was both a romantic idol and a brilliant villain in Mexican, American and European films.

Pierre Brasseur, one of France's leading bravura villains.

specifically Germany, France, Sweden, and England—have their own specialties in villainy, and it would be possible to build a quite different volume of *The Bad Guys* solely around the films—and the villains—of those countries. Each country produced a number of really unique villains who were quite the equal of our own Chaneys and Karloffs. Germany's Rudolph Klein-Rogge, a marvellously expressive actor, was a special favorite of Fritz Lang and played the menace in most of his films—ranging from Attila the Hun in *Kriemhild's Revenge*, to the crazed scientist Rotwang in the futuristic *Metropolis*. In any list of the "Top Ten" villains from *any* period and any country, Rudolph Klein-Rogge would be high among the leaders.

Also from Germany, came that superbly slimy and lecherous Fritz Rasp, a completely conscienceless rogue who played at international espionage or simple bank-robbing with the same effortless abandon as he assaulted the helpless blind girl in *The Love of Jeanne Ney*. Rasp was always a "little man" in crime—the

Marcel Dalio, specialist in lecherous, double-crossing, small-time gangsters, is France's own Peter Lorre; seen here with Simone Signoret in *Dédee* (1947).

None of Tod Slaughter's leading ladies ever amounted to much. They merely had to look pretty—and virginal—and leave the rest up to the redoubtable Mr. Slaughter. This is Hilary Eaves.

Britain's Tod Slaughter in *Crimes at the Dark House* (1940), an adaptation of *The Woman in White*. Receiving the *coup de grâce* is Hay Petrie.

paid underling, the go-between, the informer—going about his unsavory duties with a wink and a sneer that told audiences he had even less respect for his current employer than he had for himself, and that as soon as the opportunity presented itself, he would double-cross him!

Sweden's major contribution was Stig Jarrell, whose compelling performance in *Torment* as the sadistic schoolmaster who terrifies his pupils, and who turns out to be a pitiful, almost *pitiable*, sexual degenerate, was one of the cinematic shocks of the immediate postwar years of the 1940's. Audiences, out of touch with films from Europe, and cosily familiar with fairly normal Hollywood villains, found this distasteful yet tremendously powerful performance bringing them up with a jolt.

France, too, produced many a memorable "sick" villain—one of the most accomplished being Jules Berry. As the wheedling, over-talkative, self-apologetic heavy of *Le Jour se Leve*, an animal trainer who

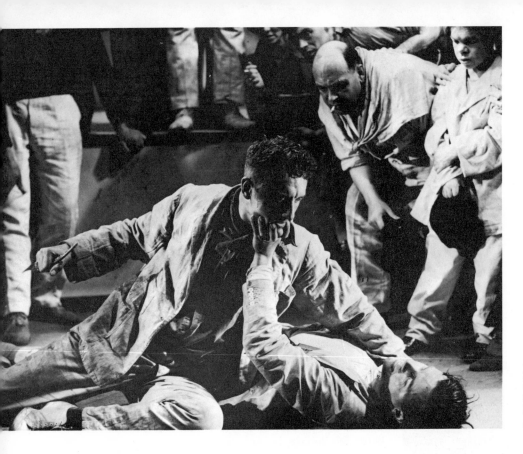

Henry Victor, an excellent villain in German, French, British and American thrillers, is shown here in *Tiger Bay*, a British melodrama of 1934.

achieves his remarkable tricks by burning the soles of his dogs' feet and flicking at them with whips during the act, and who seduces his innocent young ward and taunts the man who loves her by describing it—Berry created an uneasily convincing picture of corruption that Vincent Price was quite unable to match in the Hollywood remake, *The Long Night*.

But perhaps it is from England that the steadiest stream of villains has come—most of them, like Karloff and Rathbone, streaming straight to Hollywood. The best of the more recent British villains, Anthony Dawson, an accomplished actor who has also turned to directing, has successfully managed to combine the suavity of Rathbone with viciousness and a suggestion

Ralph Richardson provided a magnificently wild and woolly satire of the Professor Moriarty brand of villain in *Bulldog Jack* (1935), starring British comic Jack Hulbert. Fay Wray is the lady in distress as the British Museum is looted.

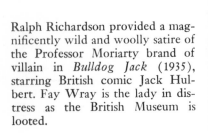

Richardson and Jack Hulbert fight it out over the live "third rail" on London's subway.

of the psychotic. The extroverted degenerate of *The Long Dark Hall* and the nuclear spy of *Valley of the Eagles* were followed by a sojourn on the New York stage in the fabulously successful mystery play *Dial M for Murder*, and thence a trip to Hollywood to re-create the role in Alfred Hitchcock's film version. Dawson's role as the cashiered Captain Lesgate, no longer an officer, but clinging to the remnants of being a gentleman, reluctantly blackmailed into becoming a hired killer, suited Dawson down to the ground. His notable villainies since then, both in Britain and America, have been as the debauched and palsied old nobleman in *Curse of the Werewolf*, and as red-herring menaces to Doris Day and Hayley Mills respectively

Peter Reynolds, right (with Patrick Holt in *Guilt is my Shadow*, 1949), was, for a while, groomed as a British Richard Widmark in giggling-killer roles.

119

Robert Newton, a sophisticated modern villain or a rip-roaring swashbuckler, was one of Britain's best heavies. From *Obsession* (1949).

Peter Bull, grim and gross, is an uncompromisingly unpleasant and disgusting heavy.

Raymond Lovell as Dr. Winkler in *Alibi* (1941)—a British remake of a famous French thriller that had starred Erich von Stroheim.

Eric Portman, left, for years an unnoticed British actor, vaulted to fame with his performance as the vicious Nazi "superman" in *49th Parallel* (released in the U.S. as *The Invaders*) in 1941. His associate is John Chandos; his captive, Leslie Howard.

Harry Baur, a French equivalent of Paul Muni, like Muni mixed colorful villains in with character roles. From *Rasputin* (1938).

Francis L. Sullivan, a British predecessor of Sydney Greenstreet in playing the fat, cultured, self-indulging criminal, with Richard Widmark in *The Night and the City* (1950).

121

William Sylvester with Sandra Storme in *The Yellow Balloon* (1953), a British equivalent of the classic American thriller *The Window*.

in *Midnight Lace* and *Tiger Bay*. Dawson is quite one of the best of the newer villains, and it is a great pity that the Rathbonian brand of villainy in which he excels—from *Captain Blood* to *Love from a Stranger*—is so absent from the screen today.

British "brutes" were never too convincing. Their innate breeding invariably gave them away. But Britain did come through with a superb combination of mad killer-bedroom marauder-criminal mastermind in the splendid person of Tod Slaughter. On stage and in film, Slaughter specialized in the old Victorian melodrama like *Crimes at the Dark House* (from *The Woman in White*), *Sweeney Todd, the Demon Barber of Fleet Street*, and *The Crimes of Steven Hawke* (where he played a seemingly lovable old gentleman who was also a notorious criminal known only as "The Spine-Breaker"). Slaughter relished his villainy

Herbert Lom, one of the more colorful British character villains, whose heavies have ranged from psychiatrist-killers to gangsters and the Phantom of the Opera. This scene is from *Portrait from Life* (1949).

122

Anthony Dawson, one of the foremost British villains of recent years.

Dawson in his best screen role: as Captain Lesgate, with Ray Milland, in *Dial M for Murder* (1954).

Kenneth Griffith, who started as a seedy wastrel in British films, more interested in seduction and mild blackmail than in outright crime, has in recent years been developing into an English equivalent of Elisha Cook Jr. In *Payroll* he comes to a literally sticky end, much as Cook had done years earlier in *Dark Waters*.

to the utmost, chuckling with delight at his own horrendous crimes, making a determined assault on the virginity of every young lady he met, and never letting slip any chance to make a dishonest pound. His acting—and his rich dialogue—had all the robust style and flair of the melodramas of old. He played them well enough for them to be accepted both on their own merits, or if one so chose, as uproarious comedies. By either standard, they were a thorough delight, and Slaughter quite certainly deserves to be enshrined with the immortals of movie mayhem. Certainly no other player—not even Karloff—committed as many crimes in a single picture as did the redoubtable Mr. Slaughter. Bless his heart, he was England's own Boris Karloff, Lowell Sherman, and Ernest Torrence all rolled into one!

123

# THE "ENEMY"

Walter Long (standing) and Hobart Bosworth (center), embodiments of the bull-necked Hun in *The Little American* (1917), with Mary Pickford and Jack Holt (together, right).

D. W. Griffith's great film about the Civil War and the Reconstruction, *The Birth of a Nation*, was made in 1915, or some fifty years after the end of that conflict. Because it depicts an ugly period in American history—a period that can still be conveniently forgotten, or exploited, according to the politically opportunist needs of the times—it has been a constant source of controversy. Yet, had Griffith been able to make it *during* the Civil War itself, it might have been far more inflammatory. And, ironically, it might then be regarded today as not a controversial film at all, but merely one that reflected the heated racial feelings of the time.

Two world wars, and the films made about them, have shown that the only *great* films about war have been made long after the cessation of hostilities—when there has been time to ponder, and interpret, and develop a sense of perspective. The best films about World War One—*The Big Parade*, *All Quiet on the Western Front* and *Paths of Glory*—were made in 1925, 1930, and 1953, respectively. Similarly, the best films about World War Two—*Twelve O'Clock High* and *The Battle of the River Plate*—came well after the close of the war. None of these five films had bad guys or villains in the accepted sense; and, if there was a nominal villain, he was usually on "our" side, and was a villain only because he represented some kind of military, governmental, or political callousness or corruption.

But the scores of films made *during* the wars tell a far different story. We were too close to the conflict then to really understand the issues involved, and, in any case, movie producers and writers are not always in what one might term the closest touch with reality. All that mattered was that our side won.

John Wray as the sadistic mailman turned officer, the only individual villain in *All Quiet on the Western Front* (1930), with Lew Ayres.

Whether the film involved was a serious essay on the horrors of war, an account of battle tactics, or a wild adventure romp, certain issues had to remain constant. Above all, we were wholly right and the other side totally wrong. And because we were right, there could be no doubt at all of our ultimate victory. *We* fought honestly and cleanly, but the enemy invariably used dirty and cowardly tactics, despite overwhelming numerical superiority that made such tactics rather superfluous anyway. This generalization is, of course, unfair to a handful of relatively sober, intelligent, and

125

One of the most outspoken of anti-Nazi films, the 1939 *Confessions of a Nazi Spy* featured Paul Lukas as the German agent, opposed by FBI man Edward G. Robinson.

restrained war films, but even the best of them, remembering that they had a propagandist as well as an entertainment mission, usually succumbed to a few temptations.

During World War One, which raged for several years before America's entry into it, film-makers had the difficult task of depicting a war that they knew little about in such terms as to make America's siding with the Allies seem absolutely right, and yet at the same time reassure American wives and mothers that the doughboys would be an invincible army in little personal danger. Newsreels played up the latter angle; little actual combat footage came back from the front,

Conrad Veidt as the traditional Nazi spy in *All Through the Night* (1941).

Master spy Veidt, aides Peter Lorre and Hans Schumm, lady Nazi Judith Anderson, and refugee victim Kaaren Verne, forced to carry out orders for fear of reprisals against her father in the homeland; a typical grouping from *All Through the Night*.

but there were reels and reels of scenes showing the doughboys relaxing in camp, cheerfully doing the washing, or generously handing out doughnuts and chocolate bars to refugees. For the "entertainment" films, the pattern adopted was one of shock and melodrama. The bestial Huns were depicted as looting, raping savages, swarming down on the helpless Belgian peasantry like jungle animals. The World War One atrocities were very real, but Hollywood movies of the period tended to make them the major issue of the war. If German officers were all as depicted in the movies by George Siegmann, Erich von Stroheim, Walter Long, and Hobart Bosworth, the war would have been one long orgy, and precious little military activity would have taken place! A sympathetic German in those days was rare indeed, and if one figured prominently in the plot—as Jack Holt did as the officer who rebels against the regime and escapes to America with Mary Pickford, in DeMille's *The Little American*—the director was usually smart enough to shoot an alternate version with a different hero. DeMille, on that particular film, knew that when he was finally able to release it in France *after* the war, audiences there wouldn't take kindly to a German hero, and thus in their version Holt was killed off, and Mary found happiness instead with *French* soldier Raymond Hatton!

The overdone caricature of the bestial, rapacious, bullet-headed Hun proved a boomerang, for when hostilities ceased, President Wilson himself requested that such stereotypes be removed from, or replaced in, unreleased pictures.

In the years between the wars, Hollywood learned to develop a more realistic and respectful attitude toward the German "enemy" in its retrospective films about World War One. *All Quiet on the Western Front* was, of course, told entirely from the German viewpoint. And in the air-war spectacles like *Wings*, *The Dawn Patrol*, and *Hell's Angels*, they imparted a kind of gallantry and chivalry to the enemy fighter aces under the legendary Von Richthofen. White scarves flying bravely from their helmeted heads, British, American, and German pilots did battle in the skies like knights of old—and when one went down in defeat, the victor invariably saluted, and waved a respectful farewell.

In retrospect, World War One had become rather clouded, and it—and the men who fought it—were in danger of becoming both whitewashed and glamorized

Working for the Fatherland again: Stroheim and Lorre.

Kurt Katch (center) and Nazi goons explain the advantages of the New Order to doubting American George Raft, in *Background to Danger* (1943).

World War II brought Basil Rathbone new outlets for villainy: as the Nazi in *Paris Calling* (1941) he is vamped by Free French agent Elizabeth Bergner.

Lee J. Cobb as a Nazi interrogator in *Paris Calling*.

when World War Two came along—and instantly, understanding of and respect for the "enemy" became a thing of the past. We were back to propaganda again —and if the bad guys of World War One had seemed stereotypes, they had absolutely nothing on the scoundrels who represented the Axis powers! Now the producers had *three* targets—the Italians, the Germans, and the Japanese. Since the Japanese had gotten into the act via their sneak attack on Pearl Harbor, they were in for an especially rough time!

Hollywood set up its battle lines, and conveniently separated the three enemies into distinct and iron-clad categories. The Italians were hardly ma-

ligned at all. Their war record seemed undramatically free of either atrocities or spectacular double-crosses, and, since their hearts obviously weren't in the conflict, their battle successes were few—and their defeats and retreats many. Nobody really disliked the Italians, and, in any case, Hollywood had only just gotten over years of bitter criticism for having suggested that 95% of America's gangsters were Italians. Since the Italian forces seemed to be held in contempt by the Germans, the obvious solution seemed to be to use them for comic relief—to make fun of their unwarlike attitudes when the chips were down, and to conveniently forget the previous Italian war on Abyssinia when their be-

128

Nancy Kelly likewise interrogated by Tala Birell in *Women in Bondage* (1943).

Hans Schumm, that superb comic heavy Sig Rumann, Jack Benny and Henry Victor in Lubitsch's spoof of the Nazis, *To Be or Not to Be* (1942).

havior was, to say the least, less comic and less sympathetic. The Italians, then, were quickly disposed of, and produced no bad guys of note. Fortunio Bonanova emerged as the new Italian stereotype—an officer eternally singing "Rigoletto" in a rich baritone, complaining about the inconveniences of war, forever taking the easy way out, and shrugging off his resentment of German superiors. Bonanova's performance in *Five*

*Graves to Cairo*, as the ridiculed and ignored Italian aide to von Stroheim's Rommel, was the archetype of the World War Two Italian "villain."

But there was no such dilly-dallying with the Nazis, who seemed to exist on only two levels. First, there were the high-ranking officers, Gestapo and SS men—roles made to measure for Conrad Veidt, George Sanders, Erich von Stroheim, Walter Slezak, Raymond

Massey, Carl Esmond, Otto Kruger, and Francis Lederer. And, on a lower echelon of player importance, Robert O. Davis, Henry Victor, William Von Brincken, Lucien Prival, and Lionel Royce took on similar roles. All of them of course needed their hatchet-men and goons, and here such burly Teutons as Hans Schum and Gene Stutenroth came into their own, with black gloves and rubber truncheons. In spy melodramas—both in occupied territories and on the home front—and in straight war action dramas, Hollywood's Heinies never had it so good as in the 1940's.

The World War Two German villain was unbending in his characteristics. At the highest level, he was often a man of supreme intellect and culture, placidly listening to Wagner while his storm-troopers tried to beat a confession out of the hero. He was resolutely dedicated to his cause, given to fanatic speeches, and a mastermind at keeping several jumps ahead of the opposition. But, like all Germans (according to Hollywood), he was a methodical and regimentalized man, and it was this discipline that finally tripped him up when, at the crucial moment, he was unable to outguess the less intellectual, more emotional representative of the democracies.

Two of the best such villains were George Sanders in *Man Hunt,* and a monocled Raymond Massey in *Desperate Journey.* One of the most exhilarating and action-packed of all war films, *Desperate Journey* was actually a tongue-in-cheek spoof of its own genre, something that nobody seemed to realize at the time, and Massey's Gestapo colonel was a classic study of the guttural Nazi incessantly foiled by the daredevil adventurer. The latter role was played by Errol Flynn at his breeziest, who, after embarrassing Massey and blowing up approximately a quarter of the Third Reich, commandeers a Nazi plane and grins, "Now for Australia—and a crack at those Japs!"

To give them credit, the Nazis were single-purposed in their desire to win the war. Bestial tortures were all a part of the game of course, and time out with the whips and branding irons was perfectly acceptable. Heroines, fortunately, had far less reason to be concerned for their "honor" than the heroines of World War One movies, and the rape or seduction of captured maidens just wasn't worth the time or effort to such formidable villains as Sanders, Massey, and Veidt.

However, it was quite a different story with the

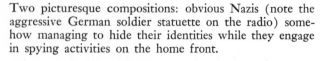
Two picturesque compositions: obvious Nazis (note the aggressive German soldier statuette on the radio) somehow managing to hide their identities while they engage in spying activities on the home front.

130

All-American Girl Gale Storm, temporarily cornered by Ivan Lebedeff (left) and Hans Schumm in *Foreign Agent* (1942).

Japanese, and Pearl Harbor enabled Hollywood to revive all the old "Yellow Peril" characteristics from the days of *The Mask of Fu Manchu*. Determined to "overthrow Western civilization," the Japanese were fanatical in battle—and Hollywood must have scoured the land to find all the wizened, apelike Japs that seemed to comprise the bulk of Hirohito's armies. (Postwar Japanese films, with their likeable young men and smiling open-faced teen-agers, were quite a revelation!) In aerial battle, there was none of the gal-lantry of the World War One dog fights. The Jap, a screaming, unshaven, wizened fanatic, crouched low over his machine guns, bombing Red Cross ships for preference, and, of course, was knocked out of the sky (by the score) by a clean-cut young American kid from Nebraska. When a movie Jap was shot down, he usually met his end screaming with fear, blood spurting enthusiastically all over his chest and face. The American pilot, killed less frequently, of course, met his end more stoically. Usually, one bullet did the trick,

Lucien Prival disarmed by Roger Pryor in *South of Panama* (1941); the girl is Virginia Vale.

Martin Kosleck, frequently cast as Dr. Goebbels.

Otto Preminger as the German villain in *Margin for Error* (1943).

William von Brincken, one of the most overworked Hollywood Prussians during the war years.

Harry Feist as the Gestapo chief, with Giovanna Galletti, in *Open City* (1945), the Italians' film slap in the face at their former allies.

An interesting publicity still of Erich von Stroheim as Field Marshal Rommel in *Five Graves to Cairo* (1943).

Many years after the war, James Mason played Rommel in a far more sympathetic light: *The Desert Fox*, 1953.

The British, too, adopted a gentlemanly feeling toward their former enemies after the war: Karel Stepanek (right) as the Commander of the *Bismarck* in *Sink the Bismarck!*, 1960.

Traditional Hollywood concepts of the lustful Jap!

efficiently and bloodlessly (as opposed to the streams of machine-gun bullets that ploughed into the Japs), and, instead of a screaming, flaming power-dive, the American plane invariably went into a slow, gradual dive, allowing time for a little patriotic theme music and reaction shots from his stern-visaged bud-

dies, who thereupon found a "personal" as well as a patriotic reason to hate the Japs. Even allowing for the propagandist motif, this lack of logic in some of the war films was astounding, and Errol Flynn's *Objective Burma* (one of the best of its type, incidentally) is a good case in point. The Japs have ambushed an American patrol, and massacred it to a man. Flynn and his men, discovering the bodies, are stunned. One man goes behind a tree to vomit. None of them can comprehend an enemy who doesn't fight openly and cleanly. Later in the film, Flynn's party discovers and surrounds an enemy troop encampment. The soldiers are off-duty, resting, sleeping, eating. By a ruse, they

134

An impressive lineup of cold-blooded Japanese militarism from *The Purple Heart* (1944), Lewis Milestone's atrocity-propaganda film.

Philip Ahn (left) and Richard Loo manhandle Ann Dvorak in *I Was an American Spy* (1951), the story of American heroine Claire Phillips and her underground activities during the Philippine occupation.

Micheline Presle also has trouble in Manila: *An American Guerilla in the Philippines* (1950).

are tricked into coming out into the open—and to a man they are slaughtered by Flynn's party—blown up with grenades, mown down by machineguns, ripped apart by knives. Afterward, Flynn congratulates his men on a job well done. The point to be remembered is that this was a routine mission, and *not* a raid undertaken in revenge for the prior massacre.

Until the postwar years, and the more restrained performances by Japanese actor Sessue Hayakawa, the Japanese military man had no redeeming features whatever. He was merciless in battle, unspeakably cruel to his captives, and, worst of all, he had **NO** sense of honor where women were concerned. In fact, many war films seemed to suggest that the whole purpose of the war was to place white women at the

Sydney Greenstreet worked overtime for the Axis in the forties; with Benson Fong in *Across the Pacific* (1942).

Japanese tong gangster from the thirties, Noel Madison becomes Japanese agent in the forties and threatens Preston Foster, Lyn Bari and the American Way of Life: *Secret Agent of Japan* (1942).

136

The movie Jap, 1942: H. T. Tsiang.

The movie Jap, 1958: Sessue Hayakawa.

lecherous mercy of leering yellow monsters! Richard Loo, Benson Fong, and Philip Ahn were the leaders in the Japanese crusade of debauchery and rape.

After the "hot" war with Japan and Germany, Hollywood found itself involved rather embarrassingly in the cold war with Russia—embarrassingly because Russia, as a former ally, had been lauded to the skies as a brave, honest, progressive nation in such films as *Song of Russia* and *Days of Glory*. Now, over-

night, everything had to be reversed. One sincerely motivated tribute to wartime Russia—*North Star*—was even taken and so recut that the Nazis of the original were now presented as the Russian aggressors, and the original Russian peasantry changed to victims of communist oppression!

The new Russian heavy turned out to be but one step removed from our old Nazi friends—he was wily, generally given more to cunning than to force, and

Hollywood cliché: Any American kid can lick *two* pint-sized Japs: *The Fighting Seabees*, 1943.

137

Japanese cliché: Japanese warriors are good-looking, dedicated and can lick any *two* Americans!

while the rubber truncheons were well in evidence, he usually got information out of his victims by such more up-to-date means as truth serums. Because communism was a more complex menace than nazism, the Russian villain talked in repetitious platitudes about "the unimportance of the individual" and other now-clichéd communist theme songs.

Initially, in the interests of diplomatic relations, the Russians were often presented as that old standby, the "unnamed" Eastern power. But, as the cold war warmed up a little, producers and writers became more outspoken. Regardless of justification, no nation *in*

*peacetime* has been so maligned by the movies of another nation as have the Russians. True, Russian movies offered distortions and lies about America (and her allies), but it was done within the standard framework of orthodox propaganda, and, in theory at least, could make little real headway since the true facts were too well known.

Hollywood, on the other hand, in some truly irresponsible moviemaking, seized on Russia and communism as a convenient scapegoat and *staple* villain, along with cattle rustlers, gangsters, and outer-space monsters. In the field of science-fiction, the Russian

The enemy master spy as a cultured, intelligent but unfeeling opponent. Leo G. Carroll (with William Eythe) in *The House on 92nd Street* (1945).

The Communist hireling is shifty, with the sort of face seen at Modern Art Museums or the unreeling of experimental movies.

became as much of a caricatured "enemy" as the Hun of old. The Communist villain of *The 27th Day* almost brings about the destruction of the entire world by meddling with, and trying to control, a number of destructive capsules sent from outer space. (All the other nations of the world play fair!) And *Red Planet Mars* really hits below the belt by having their propagandist messages re-routed through space, as though coming directly from God. In the film's incredibly tasteless climax, God Himself comes out on the side of the democracies, and brings about a religious revival,

and a corresponding destruction of communism within the Iron Curtain!

However, the *individual* villains in these films have been negligible. It is communism itself that has been the heavy, rather than its agents, and the Reds have never been as ably championed as were the Germans by Conrad Veidt and Erich von Stroheim, or the Japanese by Richard Loo and Philip Ahn. Now that the cold war seems to be thawing again, perhaps they've missed their chance for movie immortality.

One-time romantic lead Francis Lederer made a useful Nazi in the forties and fifties (and in the sixties was to play Dracula!). With Alan Ladd in one of the best of the post-war "G.I.-hunts-down-war-criminal" thrillers, *Captain Carey USA* (1950).

# THE
## SWASHBUCKLERS

It's a curious thing that while the lack of dialogue was never really a serious obstacle to the silent screen—its dramas, comedies, westerns, and fantasies could equal and often surpass those of the later sound screen—the swashbuckling costume adventure was one genre that did fare better in talkies. Somehow, dialogue was needed both to bring reality to essentially nonrealistic fare, and, at the same time, by its color and elegance, to enhance and exploit the values of escapism and theatricality.

The swashbuckling hero of the silents—and, of course, Douglas Fairbanks was the king—had less of a problem. He had his grace, his daredevil grin, and his athletic prowess all working for him. Even here

costume films as *The Sea Hawk, Scaramouche, Captain Blood,* and *Don Juan* provided the silent screen with plenty of openings for full-blooded villains. But, because of the lack of dialogue, there were really only two directions in which these villains could go. One was to play the role tongue-in-cheek, a delightful approach but by no means easy to master, and one that was to all but disappear when sound arrived. The maestros of this particular brand of villainy, Noah Beery and Montague Love, have been dealt with at greater length in an earlier chapter. The other approach, and the one usually adopted, was of full-blooded but quite serious villainy—two-dimensional scoundrels without a sense of humor or any other re-

Douglas Fairbanks vs. Robert McKim in *The Mark of Zorro* (1920).

though, it should be remembered that there was only *one* Fairbanks. Lewis Stone was a less memorable hero in the silent *The Prisoner of Zenda* than was Ronald Colman in the talkie, not because he was a lesser actor or a less impressive figure, but almost solely because Colman had the benefit of classically phrased dialogue that fitted the pomp, elegance, and bravado of the adventure like a glove.

The Fairbanks adventures, and such spectacular

Sheldon Lewis and Lucille LaVerne as the Frochards, evil brother and sister, made a fine pair of villains in *Orphans of the Storm*, 1921. Lucille's later villainy included being a model for the witch in Disney's *Snow White and the Seven Dwarfs*, which also used her voice as that of the witch.

Stuart Holmes as Black Michael, with Barbara Lamaar, in the 1922 version of *The Prisoner of Zenda*.

deeming features, and rather prone to overdo the sneer as a constant reminder to audiences that they were up to no good.

Prior to the 1920's, swashbucklers were rare on the screen. Those that were attempted were usually stiff and stagey, and it wasn't until the 1920's, and the era of the "big" picture, that the sword-and-dagger film really came into its own, both in the flowing and extravagant style so necessary to the species, and in the development of first-rate villains.

Not unexpectedly, some of the best screen skulduggery was to be seen in the huge pageants—somehow that word seems to fit them best—of Douglas Fairbanks. His *Robin Hood* of 1922 had a duo of particularly fine villains in Sam de Grasse and Paul Dickey. "Slimy" is the only word one can use in describing de Grasse. His whole being suggesting craft, cunning, and cruelty, he made an admirably loathesome Prince John. An efficient heavy in modern dress too, de Grasse was nonetheless at his best in costume roles; some five years later, he made an excellent Talleyrand (and undoubtedly an even more conniving one than history has proven him to be) in *The Fighting Eagle.* But all Robin Hood fanciers know that Robin's real nemesis was not so much the cowardly Prince John as the evil Guy of Gisbourne—and Fairbanks' film offered us a memorable portrait from a great silent screen villain now all but forgotten, Paul

Dickey. His Sir Guy was bloated, gross, treacherous, lustful, and a formidable opponent with sword or lance. And—the crowning vice in any Fairbanksian frolic—he had no sense of humor, no chivalry, no

Charles Stevens, a grandson of Indian warrior Geronimo and a mascot in all Fairbanks pictures, is once more outwitted by Doug. From *Robin Hood* (1922).

142

William Powell, much of whose early villainy took place in doublet and tights, tries to force his attentions on the young Queen, Mary Tudor (Marion Davies), in *When Knighthood was in Flower* (1922).

sportsmanship, and was a poor loser. Robin disposed of him in an appropriate manner by besting him in hand-to-hand combat, and then breaking his spine by wrapping him around a stone pillar in Nottingham Castle!

In *Don Q, Son of Zorro*, Donald Crisp (who also directed—insofar as anyone ever *really* directed Douglas Fairbanks) made an impressively sinister villain with his thin pointed beard and ultra-tight uniform. But his killing and conniving was in such deadly earnest, as opposed to the tongue-in-cheek flavor of the rest of it, that one was delighted to see Doug ultimately defeat him not by a rapier thrust but by stripping him of his dignity, and letting all the prissy pomp hiss out.

Perhaps it was for this specific reason that Fairbanks so rarely used that brand of villain (Noah Beery and Montague Love in particular) whose exuberance matched his own. Reasoning perhaps that there would be no contrast that way, and that the scales so lightly weighted toward the humorous might well overbalance into burlesque, Doug had most of his villains play it straight. Ulrich Haupt, another cold and cunning fellow in the Sam de Grasse tradition, was his heavy in *The Iron Mask*.

But, if Doug insisted on his villains taking themselves seriously, he himself rarely did—and one of the grisliest and most villainous moments in *The Black Pirate* is also one of the funniest. Some amusingly written titles set up piracy as more of a game than a crime, and we are then introduced to a group of hapless prisoners aboard a pirate ship. One of them, seeking to save some measure of his wealth, hastily removes

Brandon Hurst, an admirably slimy villain, as the betrayer of Quasimodo (Lon Chaney) in *The Hunchback of Notre Dame* (1923).

143

Marc McDermott, left, clashes with Milton Sills in 1924's *The Sea Hawk*.

a valuable ring from his finger and swallows it. But the pirate chief—dark and swarthy Anders Randolf—sees, and issues a hurried instruction to an underling. The pirate hurries off-screen, unsheathing his sword, and moments later returns, reddened sword under his arm, and the ring held in his bloody paws! Here silence was a positive asset, since it removed the barrier of reality (the victim's screams) which would have made the scene unpalatable. In Fairbanks' deft hands, and in the cheerful hues of the early Technicolor used on that 1926 production, it became a genuinely comic vignette. Anders Randolf, the pirate chief, is actually better-known as a more modern menace (for example, the sadistic husband of Greta Garbo in *The Kiss*) but with shaven head and long moustache, he made a magnificently swaggering villain in *The Black Pirate*. He "got his" early in the film in a duel sequence where Doug placed a sword, blade up, in the sand, and forced his opponent to trip backwards onto it. At this point, Randolf's lieutenant, Sam de Grasse again, took over, to come to an equally sticky end a few reels later.

Before leaving the Fairbanks films, we shouldn't overlook the considerable if unspectacular contributions of Charles Stevens. An Indian actor, and grandson of Geronimo, Stevens was a friend of Fairbanks and a mascot who appeared in just about all of his films. A better actor than he was given credit for, Stevens could appear open and friendly, but more often, with a little deft make-up, sinister and even grotesque. With minor changes in make-up, he would often play several villain bits in a single Fairbanks feature, and, in *The Black Pirate*, he could be seen getting killed as

Lionel Barrymore as the infamous Captain Walter Butler in *America* (1924).

144

three or four different pirates, one of them a genuinely sinister creation with fang-like teeth!

In his day, Stuart Holmes—the Black Michael of the silent *The Prisoner of Zenda*—was considered one of the leading screen heavies, but his villainy tends to date a little because of his lack of the cold menace of a De Grasse, or the jovial exhibitionism of a Beery. Also, because Holmes hurried back and forth between swashbucklers and westerns, burlesque villains in Hal Roach comedies, and bedroom lechers in such films as *Paint and Powder*, he never became firmly associated with any one branch of villainy, although he probably spent *most* of his time planning Ruritanian revolutions or assassinations. In fact, he was still following this line of work into the talkie era, when he was one of the noblemen in on the plot to murder boy-king Mickey Rooney in the Tom Mix western, *My Pal the King*.

Another silent-day villain whose face looked as evil as the deeds he was called upon to perform was Sheldon Lewis, erstwhile heavy of such early serials as *The Iron Claw*, and one of several who played Dr. Jekyll and Mr. Hyde. But Lewis was always best used with costume and cutlass, and seldom to better effect than in D. W. Griffith's 1921 epic of the French Revolution, *Orphans of the Storm*. As the evil brother of equally wicked Lucille La Verne, he kidnaps blind Dorothy Gish and forces her to beg in the streets for him. "You'll shiver better without that shawl!" she is told as she is forced into a snowstorm with a tin cup. Of course, Lewis has further plans for blind Dorothy too—and putting her into a rat-infested cellar is one of his methods for getting her to give in!

Donald Crisp with Douglas Fairbanks in *Don Q, Son of Zorro* (1925).

Basil Rathbone as the French pirate Levasseur, with Errol Flynn, in *Captain Blood* (1935).

Griffith's costume films produced some of the most memorable villainous portraits of the 1920's, and two of the best came from Lionel Barrymore—as the hunchbacked sadist in *Drums of Love*, and, best of all, as the infamous Captain Walter Butler in *America*. Butler, of the Cherry Valley massacres, was despised by both the British and the Americans in the Revolutionary War, and Barrymore played him with just the right mixture of charm, magnetism, fanaticism, courage, and sadism. Butler was a colorful and fascinating if ignoble character—one of history's enigmas—and Barrymore's interpretation and playing of the role was one of the best things he ever did on the screen.

With talkies, the swashbuckler died temporarily. It seemed old-fashioned, too out of tune with the more realistic demands of the Depression years. But the talkie swashbuckler and Douglas Fairbanks' successor, Errol Flynn, came to the screen simultaneously in the mid-1930's. And they brought with them probably the best all-around villain the movies ever had—Basil Rathbone. He had been in films since the late 1920's, but it was his period villainy in the mid-1930's that really brought him to prominence. Adept at any kind of role, including romantic drama and comedy, Rathbone was at his best in villainy (including modern wife-killers and Nazis) and was absolutely unmatched at playing swaggering scoundrels of other days, where his rich delivery of full-blooded dialogue, while attired in doublets or court finery, made him truly a sight to behold—and to listen to. The roles he played between 1935 and 1940 read like an honor roll of classic movie villains. He was Sir Guy of Gisbourne

As Tybalt, Rathbone delivers a death thrust to Mercutio (John Barrymore) in *Romeo and Juliet* (1936). Leslie Howard and Reginald Denny look on.

Rathbone's finest screen villainy: as the stepfather of young Freddie Bartholomew in *David Copperfield* (1935).

Rathbone's villainy continued un-abated in *The Adventures of Marco Polo* with Sigrid Gurie. This time he was dispatched not by Errol Flynn but by Gary Cooper.

Rathbone as the evil Guy of Gis-bourne is once again about to get his just desert from Errol Flynn's blade: *Adventures of Robin Hood*, 1939.

to Errol Flynn's Robin Hood, and a conniving Don Sebastien to Tyrone Power's Zorro—both of these films having beautifully staged duelling sequences. He had the handsome features that could understandably beguile an innocent maiden, and the athletic ability to prove a real opponent to his swashbuckling heroes. And, if a little ham crept into his roles occasionally (especially his French pirate Levasseur in another fine Flynn adventure, *Captain Blood*), well, the roles were all the better for it. It is only the really great actors who can get away with a little deliberate ham now and then. Away from Flynn and Power, Rathbone's flair for costume villainy was amply demonstrated in three films for MGM—as Tybalt in *Romeo and Juliet* he killed John Barrymore in a duel before being himself

despatched by Leslie Howard; in *A Tale of Two Cities*, he was one of the more sinister undercurrents of the French Revolution.

In another Dickens-based movie, *David Copper-field*, he gave perhaps his most villainous performance of all. As Mr. Murdstone, who first charms the young David's widowed mother into marriage and then, with his sister, proceeds to make her life a living hell with his coldness, sadism, and puritanism, Rathbone had one of the smaller but most effective parts of his career. Shorn of the moustache that gave even his most cold-blooded villains a kind of daredevil charm, he was able to utilize his thin lips to chilling effect, especially in the almost unbearable scene where he whips David. (Incidentally, the scene is made "un-

147

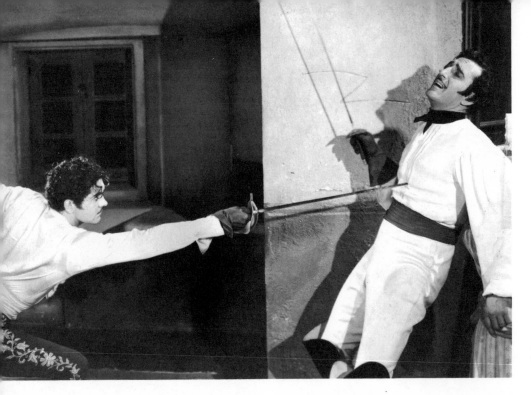

Another death thrust: this time by the hand of Tyrone Power in *The Mark of Zorro*.

bearable" not by any physical brutality, which is at a minimum, but by the skill of the two players—Freddie Bartholomew with his childish innocence, honesty, and wistfully appealing face, and Rathbone with his obvious determination, against which all entreaties are useless, to vent his sadistic spleen on the child.) As David unwittingly, and in terror, bites his stepfather, Murdstone steps back with obvious relish at the new excuse this gives him. "Ahah, he bites!" announces the delighted Murdstone, who proceeds to tell David that he is about to make him "wince and whimper." In all of his career, Rathbone never really topped this moment.

His last outstanding brush with the historical villain came in 1939 when he played Richard the Third with cool venom in *Tower of London*. A script that played as much for horror as for subtler menace teamed him with Boris Karloff, much as Bela Lugosi might have been teamed a few years earlier, but it did provide Rathbone with one of his biggest and longest classic villain roles. Thereafter, Rathbone was—and still is—continually active in screen villainy, but with the grace and agility of his younger days now well behind him, obviously a Guy of Gisbourne or a Levasseur is no longer possible. We should be grateful indeed that such a cycle returned to the screen when he was at his personal peak.

Rathbone had no serious rivals in his field—none at all in the realm of known box office players—but on a slightly more stolid and less athletic level a too often underrated actor, Henry Daniell, provided some out-

Although a romantic idol, John Barrymore played many a rascal and villain. *Svengali* (1931) was one of his best.

148

Pancho Villa (Wallace Beery) and President Madero (Henry B. Walthall) are unaware of the betrayal planned by a scheming general—played by Joseph Schildkraut: from 1934's *Viva Villa*.

The movies—and Charles Laughton—made an arch-villain out of the much maligned Captain Bligh. From 1936's *Mutiny on the Bounty*. Another familiar film villain, Stanley Fields, is at extreme right.

Laughton as the villainous squire who heads a band of shipwreckers in *Jamaica Inn* (1939).

Henry Daniell and Greta Garbo in *Camille* (1936).

standing performances, quite the equal in their own way of Rathbone's. His dignified mien, his clear diction (and his cleverly overbearing use of both of those assets) made him a master in the realm of supercilious villains—in some ways, even the superior of Rathbone since there was nothing of the ham in his performances, which were always uncomfortably convincing. Daniell was at his finest in *Camille* as the sadistic nobleman who is Garbo's "protector," and who takes delight in publicly degrading his former mistress. As an agent for Spain during the Inquisition, he made a worthy foe of Errol Flynn in *The Sea Hawk*, was likewise a grim emissary for Oliver Cromwell against Douglas Fairbanks Jr. in *The Exile*, and, in one of his best performances, won audience sympathy for the grave-robbing doctor in *The Body Snatchers*. Daniell, like Rathbone, was equally at ease with contemporary villainy too. He was one of the best Professor Moriartys in the Sherlock Holmes films (pitted, ironically, *against* Rathbone) and brought a sardonic, superbly underplayed sense of humor to the role of Garbitsch (a take-off on Goebbels) in Chaplin's *The Great Dictator*. But it was in *Camille* and *The Sea Hawk* that Daniell left his most indelible mark.

The other great sound-era villains within the genre resolve themselves, for the most part, into a series of individually outstanding performances by players who by no means specialized in such roles. Douglas Fairbanks Jr. as Rupert of Hentzau in *The Prisoner of Zenda* was the very apotheosis of the dashing, devil-may-care scoundrel—sympathetic by virtue of his charm and daring, regardless of the crimes (including murder) concealed by that smiling exterior. Yet, Fairbanks followed through with no similar villainy.

Raymond Massey as Black Michael, with Mary Astor, in the 1937 version of *The Prisoner of Zenda*.

150

One of George Sanders' best costume heavies was in *The House of Seven Gables* (1940) with Vincent Price and Margaret Lindsay.

In that same *Prisoner of Zenda*, Raymond Massey was superb as the monocled Black Michael, and, in *The Drum* was almost as good as the Indian prince, who seeks to rouse the tribesmen to revolt, and gloatingly tells of "the white English throats ready for the knife!" Yet, one can scarcely file away in a villain category the actor who is best remembered for his Abraham Lincoln and John Brown portrayals.

From piracy (*The Black Swan*) and slave-running (*Slave Ship*) to period melodrama (*Son of Fury*) and sophisticated degeneracy (*The Picture of Dorian Gray*), George Sanders has worn period finery with distinction and conviction—but somehow his insolent, dry wit has made his villainy more suited to the 20th century than to the 18th.

And, from Captain Bligh to Captain Kidd, Charles Laughton has offered some memorable portrayals of costume villainy, but his forte, too, was essentially in the modern world. However, it is interesting that his dynamic and stylized playing of Captain Bligh in *Mutiny on the Bounty* (and his superb reading of classic dialogue) transformed that stern but efficient seaman

Sanders plays pirates with Tyrone Power in *The Black Swan* (1942).

George Sanders, ably assisted by Lionel Royce (right) in *The Son of Monte Cristo* (1940).

*The Corsican Brothers* (1941), another Dumas adventure, saw Douglas Fairbanks Jr. as the hero, Ruth Warwick as the heroine, and Akim Tamiroff as a swarthy and sadistic villain.

One of the highlights of the forties was Kurt Katch's magnificently evil Mongol Khan in *Ali Baba and the 40 Thieves* (1944), seen here with Frank Puglia (right).

152

Edward Arnold as the evil Wazir in the 1944 version of *Kismet*, with Marlene Dietrich.

Orson Welles (as Cesare Borgia), with British villain Leslie Bradley, in *The Prince of Foxes* (1949) with Tyrone Power.

British actor Robert Douglas, one of the few worthwhile successors to Rathbone, fights it out with Errol Flynn as Viveca Lindfors watches in *The Adventures of Don Juan* (1948).

153

Robert Douglas as Black Michael, and James Mason as Rupert of Hentzau, in the 1952 version of *The Prisoner of Zenda*.

into one of the super-villains of all time so far as movie audiences all over the world are concerned. Pages of meticulous documentation exist to show that Bligh in fact was far from the brutal sadist depicted by Laughton—but one hundred and twenty minutes of stirring movie-making have quite overshadowed volumes and volumes of historic record!

In more recent years, the swashbuckling adventure film has become more and more of a staple ingredient, almost as commonplace as the western. And it has been cast accordingly, with the principal villains (George Macready being a particular case in point) being merely borrowed from their accustomed stamping grounds in contemporary crime, while their henchmen—Ray Teal, Harry Cording—still spoke and acted like the rustlers or land-grabbers that they usually

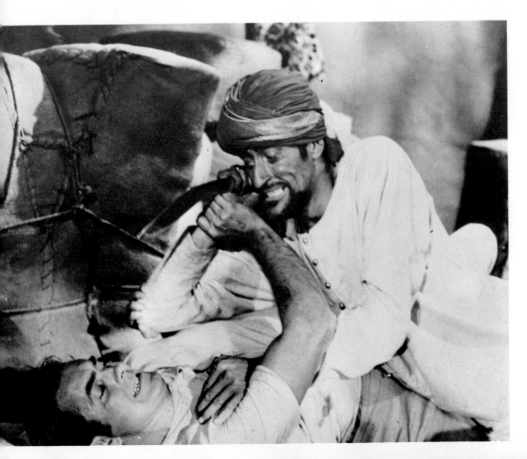

Guy Rolfe with Tyrone Power in *King of the Khyber Rifles* (1953).

Jack Palance in *The Mongols* (1962).

played in cheap westerns. Except for an occasional foray into the field by a James Mason (who made a fine Rupert of Hentzau in the most recent *The Prisoner of Zenda*) or a Mel Ferrer (a fine villain in *Scaramouche*, one of the best and most stylish swashbucklers of the past two decades), the cloak-and-sword field has become notably bereft of the necessary personalities. Douglas Fairbanks Sr., John Barrymore, Errol Flynn, Tyrone Power, Henry Daniell, Montague Love, Noah Beery, Charles Laughton, Ronald Colman, Lionel Barrymore, and Sam de Grasse are all gone now. In fact, all that remain of a once-great dynasty of chivalrous heroes and dastardly villains are Douglas Fairbanks Jr. and Basil Rathbone—hardly sufficient to sustain any renaissance of the genre. And yet, at that, these two old pros could still show the newcomers a thing or two!

Trevor Howard (right) as a rather different Captain Bligh in 1963's remake of *Mutiny on the Bounty*, with Marlon Brando.

# THE HOODED
## KILLERS

A 1919 Batman intervenes as Ben Wilson throttles another villain in *The Branded Four*.

Perhaps the most endearing of all movie villains were those who exhibited showmanship and a decided flair for the dramatic by concealing their identities from friend and foe alike behind bizarre disguises, flowing robes and headpieces, to be known only as the "Ghost" or the "Scorpion." Those were the two most popular nom de plumes, incidentally, used several times each, although we've also had such colorful aliases as the Wolf-Devil, the Professor, the Clutching Hand, the Unknown, the Octopus, the Gargoyle, the Lame One,

In 1920's *The Phantom Foe*, a fur coat was the all-concealing costume.

The Wolf Devil carries off Ethlyne Clair in *Queen of the Northwoods* (1929).

Ginger Rogers in *The 13th Guest* (1932) is attacked by a close relative whose identity remained effectively hidden until the last reel.

the Master Key, El Shaitan, the Dragon, the Lightning, Tiger Shark, and the Rattler. These worthies, and a score of others, have easily out-numbered the few masked heroes working for law and order—the Lone Ranger, Batman, the Spider, the Green Archer, the Shadow, the Vigilante, the Masked Marvel, Captain America.

Most of these colorful delinquents, creations of pulp magazines and comic strips, reached the screen via the serial. The never-ending search for their true identity lent both suspense and an element of cohesion to rambling plot lines that were strong on mystery and action but usually a trifle weak on logic.

The screen's first masked menace was almost certainly the Clutching Hand, the sinister villain of Arthur B. Reeve's Craig Kennedy stories, and the nemesis of Pearl White in one of her earlier serials, 1914's *The Exploits of Elaine*. Like all successful master-criminals, he had a massive organization behind him, was constantly outguessing his opponents, and had a thorough disdain for human life. (Throughout the years, in order to prove their omnipotence, these crime lords frequently killed hundreds and even thousands at a time, as they wrecked trains, liners, planes, dynamited dams, flooded tunnels and subways, and inundated New York with tidal waves. In the final

"The Scorpion"—black cloak and lobster claw—was the villain in *Blake of Scotland Yard* (1937). Herbert Rawlinson (center) scuffling with Bob Terry, was Blake.

The "Ghost of Treasure Island" battles Don Terry in the 1938 serial *Secret of Treasure Island*. He vanished early in the serial to lend credence to a later claim that he was merely an image thrown by a movie projector!

chapter of *The Phantom Creeps*, Bela Lugosi, zooming over New York in a tiny plane with a thin vial of his explosive formula, gleefully planned to throw it overboard and "blow up the entire world," happily unmindful that this might affect him too!) However, the Craig Kennedy of the first Clutching Hand serial was almost equally unconcerned with human life. The Clutching Hand, it seems, wants Kennedy off his trail and, with his new death ray, threatens to kill pedestrians outside of Kennedy's apartment should the detective fail to give up the case. Curiously, and with the detached interest of the true criminologist, Kennedy watches from behind his curtain at the appointed

hour. Only when pedestrians begin to drop like flies from the unseen death ray does he decide to give in to the Clutching Hand's request—or, at least, to pretend to.

To give them full credit, the masked villains of the serials were willing to undergo considerable personal discomfort to create an impression. A favorite device was to pose as a club-footed hunchback, and, draped in a black cloak, to lurch through the streets in broad daylight. This not only slowed them down somewhat, but also seemed a trifle unnecessary, since the ruse never seemed to impress the blasé and nonchalant passers-by. Such a villain was the Frog in a 1925 serial,

159

"The Lightning" (left) with assistant John Piccori (right) made life difficult for the United States Marines in *Fighting Devil Dogs*.

*Officer 444.* An astonishing introductory title informed the audience that the Frog was one of those creatures who used a cloak of infirmity to hide his diabolic crimes—which seemed to add to the already considerable burdens of "legitimate" hunchbacks by planting the suspicion that they too might be fakes and criminals! As the titles further told us every week for ten weeks, he also had "a subtle aide, the Vulture, played by Ruth Royce." But the Vulture was too subtle to

"The Octopus" (in white) gives his staff a pep talk in *The Spider's Web* (1938).

wear anything but normal street clothes, and where she got her nickname was never revealed. Most of the fun for the audience—and most of the work for the hero—was in deciding just *who* the villain really was. Good serials were quite ingenious in their red herrings, but *Officer 444* unfortunately wasn't one of them. There were never more than five suspects at most, and since three of them were obviously played by the same man with a minimum of make-up, the guessing game

A sequel, *The Spider Returns* (1941), featured an obviously related villain in *The Gargoyle*.

*Dick Tracy vs. Crime Inc.* (1941) had "the Ghost" as its rather top-heavy heavy. The henchman on the left is John Davidson.

was not so much who would turn out to be the Frog, but how long it would take the rather dense hero to catch on.

The villain's motives in the silent serial were always comfortingly direct, however, and easy to follow. The villain who wanted to "dominate the world" was still rare: most of them merely wanted to cheat the heroine out of her inheritance, corner the market on a revolutionary invention, or find a hidden treasure. The Wolf-Devil, the villain of *Queen of the North-woods,* was seemingly a little more original. He wanted to either kill or drive off all the whites in Alaska. But, in the final chapter, he was revealed to be a white man himself, a smuggler of opium who had become a drug addict.

The coming of sound brought with it dialogue (and hence more elaborate schemings and motivations) and, through the manipulation of voices, a further way to confuse the seeker after the villain's identity. However, sound also brought with it realism and the need for logic that the silent serials had done so nicely without. Of less box office value now, even though still afforded good production values, they were relegated largely to the children's market, and thus writers and directors refused to take them as comparatively seriously as they had until then. Imagination ran riot in seeking to make each supercriminal more bizarre than the one before. The extent of his worldwide organization, with spies seemingly in every law enforcement and governmental agency, was staggering to say the least. The incredibly elaborate secret rooms, machines that produced every effect from invisibility to the transmigration of souls, and torture palaces that would have delighted the Borgias, did strain the credulity a little. One wonders what must have been the reaction of contractors and builders asked to construct crocodile pits beneath the floors of Los Angeles business offices! And, the serials *never* played fair. Short in one episode, fat in another, tall in a third, the villain's stature—and voice—was never the same from one episode to the next. *Mystery Mountain*, a Ken Maynard serial, was even so unsporting as to have the mysterious Rattler played by an actor who was not in the cast,

did not otherwise appear in the serial, and who definitely was *not* the player finally unmasked. The Rattler was an especially ingenious villain in that he constructed rubber masks of all the other leading protagonists. Back to the camera, he'd put the mask on, and then, with a jump cut, Ken Maynard, Edward Earle, and other players would turn around, "adjusting" their masks! Of course, there were certain fairly reliable giveaways. When a prominent actor, usually above the histrionic standards of other members of the cast, was given third or fourth billing but seemed to have nothing to do, one had to do little more guessing. Ralph Morgan, Harry Worth, and Conway Tearle all fell into this category on occasion. Curiously, no writer was ever smart enough to exploit such foreknowledge by keeping the "name" actor in a minor role, and letting the mastermind turn out to be a lesser player. However, serial writing—often with six or more scenarists collaborating—was an erratic business, slanted for economy, the maximum usage of existing stock footage, with the knowledge that certain actors had been hired for perhaps one day only. Accordingly, it is highly probable that many serials didn't even decide on the ultimate identities of their villains until

Another "Scorpion" in 1941's *The Adventures of Captain Marvel.* The minions are Carleton Young, John Bagni and Kenneth Duncan, while the metal scorpion is a miraculous device needing several lenses to make it operate. The lenses have been split up among the members of an expedition—the most above-suspicion member of which is, of course, the hooded gentleman here.

The presumably uncomfortable and overheated villain is Don Del Oro; the film, *Zorro's Fighting Legion* (1939).

shooting was well in progress. Certainly, careless writing and inept acting did a lot to dispel the innate dignity of many an impressive hidden villain! In *The Three Musketeers*, for example, the mysterious El Shaitan, sheathed in burnoose and robes, has just issued his latest orders in impressive tones, and a henchman rushes off to carry them out. Leaving the tent, and needing further aid, this decidedly American-looking Arabian bawls into the stillness of the desert night with a pronounced Brooklyn accent, "Hey! Abdullah!"

Almost all of the "who-is-it?" serials lowered their integrity to the extent of literally cheating their juvenile audiences. Nearly always the masked man and the suspect who ultimately proved to be the masked man shared a scene or two together at the beginning of the serial—and, if the writers thought that the youngsters would forget by the time another eight weeks had elapsed, they were wrong! Another favorite, and usually unexplained, device was for the hooded villain to be shot in the arm during a fracas—and for one of the suspects (an innocent one, of course) to appear the next morning with his arm bandaged. *The Fighting Marines* flouted all laws of "decent" serial behavior shamelessly by having the suspects continually making telephones calls. After every one, there'd be a cut to the villain's secret hideway and a henchman answering the phone with a dutiful "Yes, Tiger Shark!" But, perhaps that was all part of the fun—to *know* that one was being cheated, to see through the ruses, to know when one was being led, to pit one's own honest skill against the dishonest skill of six veteran writers. And, it was a safe game, too: if one guessed wrong, one could legitimately call "Foul." But, usually one didn't, and what ecstasy when, in chapter one, one had gone on record as picking Robert Frazier and rejecting Harry Worth, Stanford Jolley, Montague Shaw, and Edwin Maxwell, to be thoroughly vindicated in chapter fifteen!

"The Crimson Ghost" (1946) experiments on one of his captives (Kenneth Duncan), aided by Clayton Moore—well before he became the Lone Ranger on TV and later in movies.

# THE COMIC
# VILLAINS

Ford Sterling, perennial burlesque villain of the early Sennetts.

ing, he told the audience his plans in detail, scowled, smacked his lips in glee, looked furtively around to make sure that only the audience had heard him, lent emphasis by pounding his fist, and then hopped off to put his plan into operation.

This sharing of a confidence with the audience was a wonderful comic gimmick, although it took the nonvillainous use of the device by Laurel and Hardy to bring it to its most effective utilization. (The recent *Tom Jones* used the device well too.) Having thus pantomimed the planned crime, the execution of that crime naturally had to top it. Again, the answer was in exaggeration. Ford Sterling, Wallace Beery, Edgar Kennedy, and other Sennett heavies drew strongly on the old Victorian melodramas, with such situations as tying the heroine to the railroad tracks. Actually, although this is often considered one of *the* stock melodramatic situations of early movies, I have *never* seen it done except as a burlesque of earlier traditions of melodrama. Heroines may have fallen unconscious on the tracks, or had their feet jammed between the rails by accident, but being *strapped* to the tracks by the villain was purely and simply a comic device, and the byplay made sure that the audience knew it. When Ford Sterling tied Mabel Normand to the tracks in *Barney Oldfield's Race for Life*, he rammed the rivets and chains tight by hitting them with an outsize mallet.

The art of comic villainy is one of the most difficult of all—which is perhaps why the list of really great "funny heavies" is so small. Such a villain has the difficult task of making an audience laugh (while not alienating it as much as a normal villain would do) by secondary gags—since obviously the best ones would go to the hero.

Initially, and until true sophistication came to the screen comedy (a date we might arbitrarily put at 1916, when Chaplin began making his comedies for Mutual), there was only a thin dividing line between the serious menace and the comic one. Paul Panzer's villainy in *The Perils of Pauline* seems dated and funny today because of its reliance on the purely physical, and on its stress of gestures, facial grimaces, and pantomime.

The comic villains of Sennett's Keystone films used the same basic approach, but with a difference. They burlesqued what was already an exaggeration, and stressed its unreality by taking the audience into their confidence. Ford Sterling was Mack Sennett's principal burlesque villain, with traditional top hat, spats, and thin beard or handlebar moustache. When villainy was on his mind, the audience knew it: in close-up he'd "tell" the audience just what he was going to do. No matter that there was no sound, and that the briefest subtitle might condense what he was say-

Top hats, beards and bombs—trademarks of the early heavies. These unbilled villains are menacing (in trunk) Sydney Chaplin.

Fortune-hunter Wallace Beery tries to dazzle heiress Gloria Swanson in the 1917 Mack Sennett satire, *Teddy at the Throttle*.

And in *Teddy at the Throttle*, when Wallace Beery does likewise to Gloria Swanson, he takes out his watch, checks the arrival time of the train, and, with a chuckle, heads for the underbrush to witness the climax of his murderous plan.

The really great comic villains rarely stayed in that line for long. Chaplin, for example, made a most effective "city slicker" villain in some of his early Keystones—and of course in the feature *Tillie's Punctured Romance*. He learned the tricks of the trade too fast to want to remain a villain, but these early roles were interesting forerunners of his Landru role in his much later talkie *Monsieur Verdoux*. Oliver Hardy also was initially a burlesque villain in the wild slapstick two-reelers of Larry Semon. But, somehow, his perplexed stares at the audience, the way he manipulated his rotund form, his flourishes, and his jovial gallantry made him all too likeable a heavy.

Perhaps the finest of the early comic heavies—and the word heavy here is particularly appropriate—was Eric Campbell, a sadly neglected and underrated clown, and one of the most valuable members of Chaplin's Mutual troupe. Campbell was the huge, bull-necked villain in most of these—and, if always not an actual villain, certainly the principal nuisance. His large eyes made to seem even more fiery and menacing by the deliberately excessive use of black make-up, Eric Campbell was Chaplin's rival for Edna Purviance in *The Rink*, and, most notably of all, was the hoodlum boss in one of the funniest of all Chaplin shorts, *Easy Street*. Because his huge frame made him such an obvious choice for "bully" roles, audiences often regarded him as merely a foil for Charlie—and missed a lot of the genuine subtlety of his pantomime. He might well have developed into a great character-actor-comedian, as, in different ways, Wallace Beery and Louis Wolheim did, but he died suddenly, in an automobile accident, while his career was still in its embryonic stage at Mutual.

Many comedians deliberately cultivated their own permanent villains. The great Harry Langdon used Vernon Dent, another bulky comic, who was not exclusively a villain, but invariably—and effectively—

Bud Jamison (in top hat) and Albert Austin were burlesque heavies in most of Chaplin's Essanay films of 1915.

Again from Chaplin's Essanay period: Leo White (often a bomb-throwing French count!) with Chaplin and Edna Purviance.

Wallace Beery gloatingly waits for the express to run over the chained-to-the-tracks heroine.

did take whatever villains came along. Through the years, Dent, who died in 1963, was the comic foil for almost all the Sennett comedians of the 1920's, and for the Three Stooges and others well into the sound era. Over at Hal Roach, another bruiser, Noah Young, took sadistic glee in victimizing Harold Lloyd, Charlie

Charlie Chaplin triumphs over bully Eric Campbell in *Easy Street* (1917).

Kewpie Morgan (left) with Billy Bevan and Madeleine Hurlock in Sennett's *Whispering Whiskers* (1924).

Chase, and Snub Pollard. A sample Young gag: in *A Sea Dog's Tale*, Young calmly waits while Snub Pollard dons a diver's suit, and then, just as Snub lowers himself into the sea, Young calmly knocks a hole in the glass section of the helmet with a hitherto carefully concealed wrench! Buster Keaton, on the other hand, used subtler villains. In *Sherlock Jr.*, Erwin Connolly (a well-known minor character actor, usually playing harassed fathers or aloof butlers) scored one of the greatest single comic bits of all, merely by leering at the heroine, and, in one magnificently lascivious gesture, loosening his tie—a spoof of all the would-be seducers of all innocent heroines since the movies began.

Many comedians have, of course, allowed their villains to play it completely straight. The Marx Brothers, in letting Douglas Dumbrille play his villainy seriously, were not only able to outwit him, but to deflate his dignity and pomposity too, thus scoring extra laughs.

But, just as they have created some of the screen's funniest and cleverest comedy, so too have Laurel and Hardy seemed to hit on a special knack in creating classic comic villains—and in generously giving these villains some of the biggest laughs. Four players in particular stand out in a rich portrait gallery of Laurel and Hardy heavies. Charles Middleton, famous later on as the arch-villain Ming in the three Flash Gordon serials, had thin lips and a mean-looking face that made him ideal truant-officer fodder, and an enjoyably flamboyant theatricality in his delivery of lines that served him well as an outraged husband, an all-but-mad artist, or a merciless army officer. Laurel and Hardy made good use of him in all these guises.

Another favorite of theirs was the great Walter Long (whose serious villainy in *The Birth of a Nation*

Doug Fairbanks crosses swords—after a fashion—with Frank Campeau in the 1919 *His Majesty the American*.

Vernon Dent (right) was the fall guy and/or villain in most of Harry Langdon's silents for Sennett.

and other films, has been discussed previously). Long's brute strength terrorized the boys in many of their comedies, which would start off with him threatening to "twist your necks so that when you're walking north you'll be looking south," and wound up with him doing just that. In one film, the boys had been instrumental in his capture, and, after the judge sentences him to hang, Laurel tactlessly adds, "And I hope you choke!" In another variation of the same situation, Long is sentenced to life imprisonment, and Laurel protests, "Aren't you going to hang him?" In both cases, of course, Long escapes and seeks his revenge. He played most of these roles with a roguish twinkle in his eye, and a tongue clearly in his swarthy cheek.

I suspect that most of all he enjoyed his villainy in *Any Old Port*, a casual spoof of *Broken Blossoms*, in which Long's role is clearly kidding Donald Crisp's Battling Burrows in that 1919 Griffith classic.

The third great Laurel and Hardy villain was Richard Cramer. No player ever looked more like a villain. His face and frame were those of a bloated frog, and his voice, a mixture of a croak and the noise of knives being sharpened, matched his physical characteristics completely. I suspect that Cramer had little sense of humor, and that Laurel and Hardy exploited that weakness without his knowing it. He played straight villains and comic villains in *exactly* the same key. In westerns, he certainly looked the part of the

Walter Long, a first-rate straight heavy, was also an excellent comic one for Laurel and Hardy. From *Pardon Us* (1930).

James Finlayson

Henry Brandon, a later Fu Manchu, started his villainy as Henry Kleinbach playing the unspeakable Barnaby in *Babes in Toyland* (1934).

hard-hearted banker or the sadistic head of terrorist vigilantes. But, as soon as he opened his mouth, it was too much. One line of verbal villainy overbalanced his fearsome appearance, and one could no longer believe in him. Wisely, Laurel and Hardy saw that he was funniest just being himself, and never tried to force humor or gag lines on him. He glowered and grunted his way through their films from the early talkie shorts to their last feature for Hal Roach, *Saps at Sea*.

The fourth and greatest we have left till last—

James Finlayson as Mickey Finn vs. his old opponents Laurel and Hardy in 1937's *Way Out West*.

Maxie Rosenbloom, a specialist in dumb-hoodlum roles.

Alan Mowbray as he appeared in *The Villain Still Pursued Her*, a comedy of the early forties in which he kidded the old Victorian melodrama heavies.

Dignified Douglas Dumbrille usually played his villainy straight—even opposite the Marx Brothers. From the last of their MGM features, *The Big Store* (1941).

James Finlayson. Finlayson was a veteran comic who worked nonstop for both Sennett and Hal Roach, often merely a foil as the heroine's father on whom sundry indignities would be heaped, but more often as a smoothly burlesqued villain of the old school—fortune-hunter, mad doctor, crooked sheriff, corrupt politician, or confidence man. A Scotchman, he capitalized on the legendary reputation of that race by forever presenting a picture of a canny, grasping, conniving old skinflint. His sour-faced expression suggested that he lived on a diet of vinegar and pickles, and when talkies arrived, his Scottish expostulations and grunts merely added to the effectiveness of his characterization.

Although some of his funniest material did not necessarily find him as a villain (his prolonged battle with Laurel and Hardy in the silent *Big Business*, wherein they wreck his home while he retaliates by wrecking their car and "business," is about the funniest outburst of controlled savagery that the screen has ever seen), his best performances were those villainous ones where he could give completely free rein to the crafty viciousness that was so much a part of his screen

170

Henry Daniell, Billy Gilbert and Charlie Chaplin spoof Goebbels, Goering and Hitler in *The Great Dictator* (1940).

Dick Cramer, the incredibly evil villain of several Laurel and Hardy shorts and features.

Two straight menaces, Peter Lorre and Raymond Massey, played their overdone villainy for laughs in *Arsenic and Old Lace* (1944).

Charlie Chaplin as the Landru- and Bluebeard-inspired wife-murderer in *Monsieur Verdoux* (1947), with Martha Raye as one of his intended victims.

character. In one of the best Laurel and Hardy features, *Way Out West*, he was saloon-owner Mickey Finn, a satire of all the western villains from time immemorial. A cheat, a thief, an oppressor of the orphan left in his charge (heiress of a rich gold-mine that he plans to swindle her out of), Finlayson not only runs the gamut of western villainy, but runs it with incredible flourishes and side-trips into lunatic fancy. When Hardy, gallantly trying to rescue the heroine, hides in a piano, Finlayson gleefully sits down at the piano, first having ascertained that Hardy is inside, and energetically plays a fast jig, nodding with happy satisfaction every time a dull thud tells him that one of the piano keys has hit the hapless Hardy in the eye or the nose. Best of all, his leaping, bounding, leering performance re-created the classic lampoons of the old Sennett comics, complete to the full-face stares at the audience, and the knowing winks in its direction as he makes up his mind what course to pursue. His performance in *Way Out West* seems to wrap up all the comic villains of movie history into one concise and vastly enjoyable package.

One of the blackest and funniest comedies of all, 1963's *Dr. Strangelove* had Peter Sellers as a logical extension of those German master fiends, Dr. Caligari and Dr. Mabuse.

# THE SOCIAL
## VILLAINS

The Russian director Eisenstein disliked women intensely, so killed two birds with one stone by casting gross and unattractive women as his capitalist heavies. The lady above fights in the Czar's "Battalion of Death" in the 1927 recounting of the Revolution, *Ten Days that Shook the World*.

Unquestionably, the smallest group of villains also produced some of the most hated movie types. These were the villains in Hollywood's films of social protest in the 1930's and early 1940's—films dealing with evils of the Depression, with unemployment, with the inhumanity of banks, law enforcement bodies, and government agencies, with racial prejudices, and with the obstacles placed in the way of ex-convicts, immigrants, and destitute farmers.

Some of these films were produced out of the sincere desire to arouse a nation's conscience, to get something done about deplorable conditions. Many were made because the milieu of violence and unrest created a logical framework for sensationalism and melodrama, and because the record showed that films that could be advertised as "honest" and "outspoken" often did a little better at the box office, provided they contained a few of the standard ingredients of popular appeal as well.

The villains in these films were not villains in the sense that they killed or robbed. They were the corrupt politicians who schemed to cheat the "little people"—as for example, Edward Arnold and Claude Rains in Frank Capra's *Mr. Smith Goes to Washington*. They were the crude, coarse illiterates who refused to give an obviously intelligent and deserving man a job because he happened to be a foreigner. They were the law enforcers who saw a chance for self-aggrandizement and promotion by selecting a scapegoat and getting a popular "guilty" vote regardless of the man's probable innocence—Claude Rains again, in one of the best films on prejudice and lynch rule, 1937's *They Won't Forget*.

These villains were hateful because these films had a message to get across, and they were merely instruments for the delivery of that message. As in most

Adrian Morris, the callous, unfeeling police official who harasses the "Okies" in *The Grapes of Wrath* (1940).

Harry Woods (left) and David Landau (center) as the coarse, illiterate chain-gang supervisors in the 1932 classic *I Am a Fugitive From a Chain Gang*. Jack LaRue is the prisoner.

propaganda films (unfortunately), subtlety was usually dispensed with in favor of hard and certain impact. There were no redeeming or humanizing features about these villains. The gas-station owner who refuses to help ex-convict Henry Fonda in *You Only Live Once* is not just a rude and unfair individual. He is gross, coarse, and untidy; his girth suggests that he is well-fed and comfortably off (without really deserving it); and his whole attitude is so energetically antagonistic as to be quite unrealistic. Such types are only a stone's throw from the stylized villains of the Russian propagandist films of the 1920's. All of the "capitalist" villains—e.g. the landowners—in Eisenstein's *The General Line* are fat, gross, and are photographed from extremely low angles to emphasize their fat bel-

lies and their lordly postures, and from the rear, in close-ups of fat, perspiring, bull-necks. Eisenstein was a brilliant film-maker, and unquestionably these sledgehammer symbolisms worked on the peasantry of his own country, but such tactics introduced into the more realistic milieu of an American Depression-era film served only to irritate. They did succeed in creating hateful individuals: audiences reacted *against* them, and, because the "crimes" were those of attitudes rather than of deeds, those same audiences were also able to feel a little smug, knowing that under the similar circumstances that might easily involve them one day, they would be far more charitable. But to more discerning audiences, the hate was doubleedged. They disliked this caricature because they knew

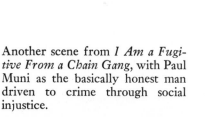

Another scene from *I Am a Fugitive From a Chain Gang*, with Paul Muni as the basically honest man driven to crime through social injustice.

Claude Rains as the politically ambitious district attorney in *They Won't Forget* (1937).

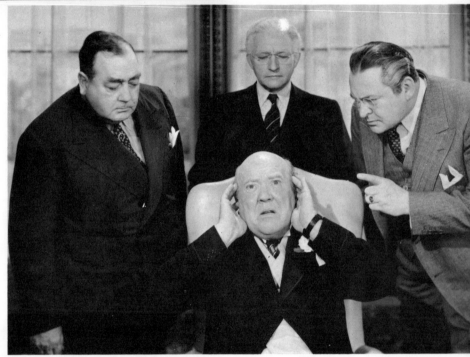

Typical Frank Capra villains from *Mr. Smith Goes to Washington* (1939). Shrewd and corrupt politicians Eugene Pallette, Claude Rains and Edward Arnold gang up on equally corrupt—but dumb—Guy Kibbee.

that beneath it all there was an element of real and unpalatable truth. But they also knew that they, the audience, were being *used;* that their natural emotions and feelings were being exploited, and that they were being *made* to hate.

Few outstanding individual villains emerged from these films for the simple reason that, aiming at an at least superficial documentary realism, the tendency was to shy away from faces too readily associated with stock types. Thus, Charles Lane, hawk-nosed, rat-faced, thin-lipped, the perennial "unpleasant" lawyer in scores of comedies and dramas, forever bursting into offices, dumping his brief case on a table, opening it, delivering his uncompromising ultimatum, and then withdrawing without giving his victim any chance for

rebuttal, was never used in the important "social" films merely because he was too closely associated with the theatrical shyster. On the other hand, equally type-expressive, yet less familiar faces, could be tremendously useful. Ward Bond, in the 1930's *not* a well-known player, was invaluable as the agitator, the lout spouting racial venom, the lynch-mob leader. Likewise, Tom Tyler, a western star of the 1920's and 1930's, and a face not likely to be too familiar to the patrons of "message" pictures, was ideal in a brief part as a vicious cop who resents the Oklahoma paupers invading California in *The Grapes of Wrath*.

Very few of the many social films of the 1930's and 1940's *really* hold up today, and it's not just because their message is, in many cases, no longer so ur-

176

gent. Fritz Lang's *You Only Live Once*, and especially the social comedies of Frank Capra, date deplorably because they are so "loaded" in their unbelievably vicious villains, and their sickeningly virtuous heroes. James Stewart in *Mr. Smith Goes to Washington* today seems far more ludicrous than the at least well-organized corrupt politicians who seemed to be vilified because they were using their status to gain personal profits as *well* as decided benefits for the state. (With the rather confused ethics and moralities of that film, I'm still not convinced that the state was better served by following the altruistic small potatoes of the bumbling Mr. Smith!)

The best social films of the 1930's, and those that retain their greatest impact, are those which, like *They Won't Forget*, offer a minimum of individual villains. True, Claude Rains is a political opportunist who railroads a probably innocent man. He is also charming, intelligent, and has used his cunning before for good, but in the same way as he is using it now for ill. But above all, one *believes* that this kind of man exists, and behaves in this way. In films that, after all, *have* to convince you of their innate truth, and seek to persuade you to do something, however small, to prevent the repetition of such injustices, such belief is of paramount importance. It hardly matters here that one hates Rains' villain far less than the gas-station attendant in *You Only Live Once*.

The classic Capra triangle: dishonest politico (Claude Rains) uses his beautiful daughter (Astrid Allwyn) and luxurious home to try to sway 110% honest hick politician James Stewart, in *Mr. Smith Goes to Washington*. But it's newspaper gal and woman-of-the-people Jean Arthur who wins him in the end.

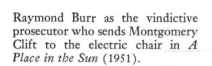

Raymond Burr as the vindictive prosecutor who sends Montgomery Clift to the electric chair in *A Place in the Sun* (1951).

# THE CIVILIZED
## HEAVIES

Perhaps the most civilized (outwardly!) of all movie scoundrels: George Arliss as the Rajah of Ruhk in *The Green Goddess* (1922), a film he remade, with the added joy of his superbly delivered dialogue, in 1929. Alice Joyce (right) was the lady very much in distress in both versions.

Just as the silent era had somewhat of a monopoly on the jovial rogues who enjoyed villainy for its own sake, so did the talkies produce their own unique brand of villain—the polished, debonair, smooth-tongued scoundrel who, thanks to a sound-track and good script-writers, used witticisms and epigrams to put the hero in his place. Rarely if ever would he

Lionel Barrymore's sardonic villainy in *Love* (1927) somewhat overshadowed Garbo, so he was completely eliminated and his scenes reshot.

His customary sartorial elegance only partially lost to the ravages of a typhoon, John Miljan, left, plots a mutiny in *The Yankee Clipper* (1927), with the assistance of a less subtle heavy, Walter Long.

stoop to gunplay or other violence himself, although he was usually smart enough to have a couple of trigger-happy goons on hand for such emergencies. And, while they systematically beat the hero to a pulp, the cultured villain would charmingly purr such lines as "I do so deplore the vulgarity of physical violence" or "How I wish you wouldn't force me to such extreme measures, when there are so many more pleasant ways to settle our little differences."

These ingratiating fellows began to appear in the early 1930's, when the mystery and detective stories started to hit the screen in ever-increasing numbers, and enjoyed a flowery and ultra-articulate vogue until the late 1940's. Then, with television turning out the half-hour mystery film en masse, more worthwhile and literate detective essays on the theater screen be-

came seemingly old-hat, and in any event commercially dubious, and the vastly enjoyable if theatrical villains exemplified by Sydney Greenstreet as Mr. Gutman in *The Maltese Falcon* were seen no more.

The loquacious and self-indulgent villains obligingly split themselves into two parallel camps: those like Sydney Greenstreet and George Sanders who made no secret of their crimes, and in fact revelled in them; and conversely, those like Otto Kruger and James Mason whose crimes, whether for profit or patriotism, were in deadly earnest. These gentlemen usually used their veneer and their apt use of a phrase as a cloak to hide their true nature.

In passing, we shouldn't neglect a small, untypical but nevertheless important group—the "unknown" killers of the mystery films whose identities were

Lawrence Grant as the well-spoken but thoroughly unspeakable villain vs. Ronald Colman's "Bulldog Drummond" of 1929.

never revealed until the climactic reel. The perennial denouement of the old Warner Oland Charlie Chan films was for the Chinese detective to gather all the suspects in one room, and systematically break down all the evidence and clues via astonishingly quick and concise deductions until ultimately he reached the end of the line and intoned, without too much triumph since he was so used to it by now, "And so *you* are murderer!" At which point, the accused, without a thought of denial or of trying to brazen it out, would rasp, "Very clever, Mr. Chan!" and try, unsuccessfully, to make his escape. Needless to say, the killer thus chosen was usually the one person never under suspicion because of his consistent and unfailing charm, cheerfulness, and willingness to cooperate. Through the years, and by no means just in the Charlie Chan movies, such character comedians as Franklyn Pangbourne, Olin Howland, and Hobart Cavanagh, and such likeable young men as Robert Kent, Robert Paige, and Reginald Denny, have turned out in the last reel to be "murderer." Since they were deliberately cast because they were *not* villain types, the many players in this category hardly warrant a detailed breakdown, and we merely salute their deceptive chicanery in passing.

But, to revert to our two basic groups. Of the "obvious" villains, there can surely be little argument in giving pride of place to Sydney Greenstreet. While it was always "obvious" that he was a master-mind villain, he managed to make it delightfully un-obvious as to whether his geniality was genuine, or whether his corruption and menace was a sham. "Perhaps I am only joking, sir!" he would remark with a bland, expressive gesture—having presented his opponent

C. Henry Gordon and Myrna Loy in *Thirteen Women* (1932).

(Bogart or Raft) with an ultimatum. But, despite the chortle of genuine glee that invariably followed such a remark, Greenstreet's movie villains never really joked. He was a huge man, whose obesity not only quivered with every laugh, but also of itself suggested the gross self-indulgence of a man who lived for pleasure—and to whom crime, whether it be for wealth or for power, was very much a part of that pleasure. The part of Gutman, "the fat man" of Dashiell Hammett's thriller *The Maltese Falcon*, was made to measure for Greenstreet. With few variations, he played that part in all his successive movies too—and

A deleted scene from *The Most Dangerous Game* (1932); Count Zaroff (Leslie Banks) with the special coffins (engraved "TO A GAME LOSER") that he keeps for his victims.

181

Bernard Nedell, oozing polish and politeness, threatens Henry Edwards in *Call of the Sea* (1935).

Jameson Thomas and Frank Conroy, two of the most gentlemanly of villains, come under the suspicion of Warner Oland in *Charlie Chan in Egypt* (1935).

Warner script-writers realized the effective contrast not only of teaming him with Peter Lorre (as a kind of unholy Laurel and Hardy) but of pitting him against laconic, direct men of action like Bogart and Raft. Greenstreet would open his sinister cat-and-mouse game with a flowery speech, a nostalgic remembrance, and a funny story. Bogart would retort with an unimpressed "What's in it for me?," and Greenstreet's next line—"Ah, a man after my own heart. To be sure, sir, let's get down to business!" would get the whole uneasy alliance of mutual mistrust under way. Even in lesser material, Greenstreet was a joy to behold; at his best, in *The Maltese Falcon, Across the Pacific* and *Background to Danger*, he was unmatched.

182

Roland Young as the unctuous Uriah Heep in *David Copperfield* (1935), with Madge Evans.

John Miljan (left) and Frank Reicher, two perennial smoothies, as political opportunists in *Sutter's Gold* (1936).

Even those who preceded Greenstreet in movies —as for example Dudley Digges, who played the Gutman role in the first version of *The Maltese Falcon*— seem now to fit into what must be termed "a Greenstreet category." This is especially true of Edward Arnold, not strictly a villain, yet responsible for a fine array of shady lawyers and high-powered crooks just the same; Gene Lockhart, who was unsurpassed in roles where his veneer finally crumbled and he wound up cringing in a corner; George Sanders, who brought an added touch of sardonic degeneracy to his heavies (especially in an unusual little "B," *Quiet Please, Murder*); and Morris Carnovsky, Luther Adler, Thomas Gomez, and George Coulouris, who never quite

Basil Rathbone as the wife-murderer in *Love From a Stranger* (1937).

J. Carroll Naish (left) and William von Brincken (right) flank Inspector Nielsen of the Yard (H. B. Warner), who keeps a traditional stiff upper lip in *Bulldog Drummond in Africa* (1938).

made it into the upper brackets, but brought stylishly civilized villainy to a number of lesser movies.

During the years of World War Two, one of the foremost and most individual of the new villains was Walter Slezak. His catlike purr was both disarming and menacing at the same time, while his roly-poly features seemed genuinely friendly, even clownish. But there was always a moment in all Slezak villain roles where the mask was dropped, and the ruthless heavy, usually a Nazi, stood suddenly revealed. Lyle Bettger, a smooth, quite good-looking villain, had the happy

Apotheosis of the Greenstreet films: *The Maltese Falcon* (1941). Left to right, Humphrey Bogart, Peter Lorre, Mary Astor and Sydney Greenstreet.

knack of being convincingly charming to the ladies —and being able to summon a sudden rage or an insane light in his eye when his carefully coordinated plans went awry. Vincent Price, although later shunted off into horror films, was for a while a prominent contender for the cast-off George Sanders roles.

John Miljan, in the late 1920's, made something of a name for himself as cowardly, despicable fortune-hunters, most notably in *The Yankee Clipper*. There, he not only "carried on" with a Chinese girl, whom he abandoned when he saw the chance to marry a rich English girl, but he instigated a mutiny, hid precious water for himself (later claiming it was for the heroine) and even put a bloodied bandage around his uninjured head to spare himself the indignity of work after a typhoon had all but wrecked the ship! Miljan's handsome features and suave voice made him an ideal philanderer and polished villain in talkies too.

Lawrence Grant's dignified face and unctuous voice served him well as a villain who loved to talk about his crimes *before* he performed them. In *Bulldog Drummond*, an early talkie, he taunts the bound Drummond (Ronald Colman) by forcing his "attentions" and kisses on the helpless heroine. For this indiscretion, and since this was before the production code, Drummond subsequently kills him in cold blood! Another talkative enemy of a later Bulldog Drummond was J. Carrol Naish, expert at playing either uncultured hoods or villains positively dripping refinement. One of his most memorable moments occurred in *Bulldog Drummond in Africa*, wherein he and his cohorts have kidnapped Inspector Nielsen of the Yard, and

Walter Slezak with Dick Powell in *Cornered* (1945).

A classic pose from the thrillers of the forties. Intellectual villain Morris Carnovsky, muscleman assistant Marvin Miller, and battered hero Humphrey Bogart. From *Dead Reckoning*, 1947.

are extending to him unusually hospitable comforts. Nielsen (played by H. B. Warner) raises his champagne glass and proposes a toast: "To men without honor . . . men who have betrayed their country" and, as it goes on, Naish's charming smile fades. "We will discuss Inspector Nielsen's toast, in detail, later," he remarks, with something of a leer. It is not anticlimactic to add that the discussion consists of the good inspector being tied to a tree, while Naish whips a lion, tethered just a few feet away, into a sufficient frenzy to break the rope restraining him!

Although not so consistently a villain, perhaps Charles Laughton came closest to rivalling Sydney Greenstreet's supremacy. There was always a sadistic, Satanic edge to Laughton's villainy, coupled with a kind of schoolboyish glee that suggested that the whole thing was really quite a lark. As the mad scientist in *Island of Lost Souls*, happily and tastelessly making monstrosities by cross-breeding animals and humans, and referring casually to "certain mistakes" while he looks at an off-screen cage containing some screeching *thing*, or as the equally mad submarine commander in *The Devil and the Deep*, telling his wife (Tallulah Bankhead) "I'm going to kill you—but I can wait!," Laughton brought a wonderful exuberance to his roles. Even later, in films like *The Big Clock*, an excellent thriller of the 1940's, the now more subdued Laughton was still able to bring about a chilling balance of repugnance and yet, at the same time, sympathy for himself.

Standing quite alone in the annals of cultured movie villains is Leslie Banks' marvellous bravura per-

formance (and his first movie acting in the bargain) as Count Zaroff in the first version of the many times remade *The Dangerous Game*. The tightest, fastest sixty-eight minutes ever put on film, it was a spellbinding tale about a mad hunter who deliberately causes ships to be wrecked off his island fortress, so that he may have human game to hunt in his private jungle. Stroking the jagged scar on his forehead, sitting down at the piano to launch into a tormented concerto, Banks was every inch the detached connoisseur of killing, his every sentence a masterpiece of construction and understatement in imparting dignity and a

Clifton Webb as the acidly witty, elegant-living murderer of *Laura*, with Gene Tierney (1944).

Nobody turned out to be the "surprise" killer with more regularity than Ralph Morgan (center), here seen with Jayne Meadows and William Powell in *Song of the Thin Man* (1947).

civilized veneer to the barbaric "sport" he has devised. "It is only after the kill that man revels!," he remarks at one point, a casual cutaway to Fay Wray's heaving bosom leaving no doubt as to the revels in mind!

Unlike Messrs. Greenstreet, Banks, and Laughton, the "unobvious" smoothies who go about their crimes behind cloaks of respectability, social reform, art, or politics are more of a piece. Respectability, usually accompanied by wealth, is their common denominator. Usually they have no reason for turning to crime at all, and thus, to be convincing, they are often motivated by non-selfish ends, which invariably means spying for an unnamed foreign power. One invariably feels sorry for such fellows, not only because they are decent sorts, but because, in their ultimate confrontation with the hero, they seem to make so much more sense. In Alfred Hitchcock's wartime thriller *Saboteur*, Robert Cummings is the All-American Boy, and Otto Kruger the urbane Nazi, happily married, highly respected, giving his all to charity and war-bond drives. In their inevitable exchange of ideologies, Cummings' prattle about "the rights of the little people" seems so meaningless as opposed to Kruger's disciplined speech about a new World Order, that one is almost rooting for Kruger to get away with it.

Departures from type-casting in this field are few. Audiences used to hearing lovable and determined Edward Van Sloan intone "We must destroy it!" in

In *Johnny Allegro* (1949) George MacCready emulated our old friend Count Zaroff as a sportsman-killer, who liked to claim his victims with bow and arrow. Nina Foch is intervening on behalf of an offscreen George Raft.

Since playing wife-murderer in Hitchcock's *Shadow of a Doubt*, Joseph Cotten has returned to crime periodically. This was perhaps the high point of his antisocial conduct: killing Marilyn Monroe in *Niagara* (1953).

*Frankenstein, Dracula,* and *The Mummy* are always a little resentful when, as has happened occasionally, he himself has turned out to be using his cloak of respectability (as a scientist, a movie producer, or a college professor) to hide a criminal career. Once in a while, such a departure *does* pay off, as when Edmund Gwenn, whose usual screen "image" was a lovable one, turned up as a private detective and bodyguard in Hitchcock's *Foreign Correspondent*—only to be revealed as a cold-blooded paid assassin behind his cheerful smile and serious Cockney small-talk.

But, for the most part, whether it's Cedric Hardwicke (in *The Invisible Man Returns* and *Lured*), Herbert Marshall (*Foreign Correspondent* and *The Unseen*), Claude Rains, James Mason, Clifton Webb, Ralph Morgan, John Hoyt, or Leo G. Carroll, the pattern remains comfortingly the same. He is gracious and charming, with a winning smile. He is a gentleman at all times, quick of wit and well-lettered. He loves good music and is a connoisseur of art. He is kindly and noted for his works of charity. In short, he is obviously not to be trusted.

Lyle Betteger with Marvin Miller in *Forbidden* (1953).

# THE PSYCHOS

Since the recognition of the "psycho" as a criminally dangerous type came relatively late in the day, and since, in any event, film utilization of themes of mental illness required far more detail and dialogue than the silents were capable of, the psycho as a movie "bad guy" was almost wholly the product of the talking picture.

To be sure, there were tentative forays into the field of psychiatry even before the word was adopted into common usage. D. W. Griffith's *The Restoration* was a remarkably prophetic little film of 1909 in which an emotionally unbalanced man is shocked back into sanity via a re-enactment of the event that had unhinged his mind. But the first genuinely Freudian film —and the first authentic psycho protagonist—was in a German film of 1926 entitled *Secrets of a Soul*. Werner Krauss (the erstwhile Dr. Caligari) starred as a suddenly unbalanced husband who attempted, without apparent reason, to kill his wife. Via a long series of dreams, and psychiatric interpretations of them, his

Lionel Barrymore as the religious fanatic, the Reverend Davidson, in *Sadie Thompson* (1928). Gloria Swanson was Sadie.

After an interim version with Joan Crawford and Walter Huston, Rita Hayworth brought Sadie to the screen again in 1953, with Jose Ferrer as the unbalanced reformer whose lust for Sadie drives him to rape and suicide.

189

Probably the screen's most famous psycho: Peter Lorre in the original *M*, made in Germany in 1931 by Fritz Lang.

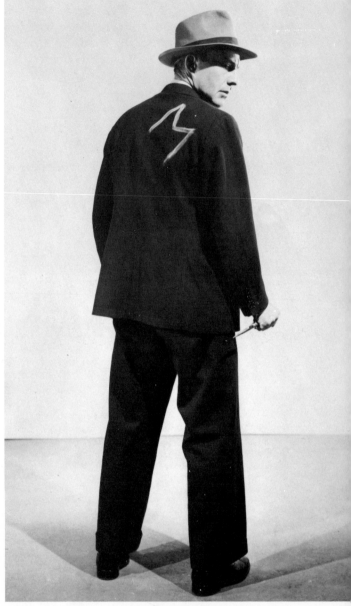

David Wayne in the 1950 American remake.

neurosis is diagnosed—and he is cured. But Freud's theories, and psychiatry itself, were still not sufficiently fashionable for the movie to start a trend.

Indeed, it was a long time before the psycho was officially inducted into the ranks of the movie badmen. Robert Montgomery's outwardly charming killer in 1937's *Night Must Fall* was very much of a psycho, but the word was not used, although in the 1964 remake with Albert Finney, far grimmer physical details —including an axe-murder in the opening sequence— stressed the killer's insanity far more obviously than Montgomery's subtler performance had done. In 1939, a comparatively unambitious crime film called *Blind Alley* created a genuine stir among critics since it brought "serious" psychiatry to the screen for the first time. Chester Morris was the cold-blooded killer troubled by nightmares; Ralph Bellamy the psychiatrist who works on his nerves until he breaks down and reveals the content of his dreams. Although the dreams were then depicted in a pictorially quite fascinating way, their content today seems quite elementary. Audiences to whom psychiatry—in movies, in novels, often in their own life—is now old stuff, have little trouble today in interpreting the symbolic meaning of Morris' nightmares long before the placid, pipe-smoking Bellamy does!

The psycho got himself a big boost in the immediate postwar years, when attention was increasingly focussed on the mental problems of maladjusted warveterans. Suddenly, movie melodramas became both intellectual and fashionable—or at least so their creators thought—by pushing unbalanced heroes *and* villains at the audience so fast that the uncomplicated villain who was mean for profit, or even just because he *liked* being mean, all but vanished. The usual procedure was to take a disturbed young man, suffering from mental blackouts, amnesia, and other mental upsets, and cause him to believe that he was guilty of murder. Gregory Peck, John Hodiak, and Robert

Cummings were three of the unfortunates who travelled that route. Usually, glamorous lady scientists, their sex appeal hidden behind glasses and severely tailored suits, proved by psychoanalysis that they were troubled by childhood memories, but were innocent of any crime. The guilty culprits (Herbert Marshall, Leo G. Carroll) invariably turned out to be the heads of the mental institutions where the hero was being treated. Shades of *The Cabinet of Dr. Caligari!*

But slowly, steadily, the genuine psycho—as a villain—was making inroads. He first appeared as the trigger-happy henchman in crime thrillers—Peter Lorre in *Desert Fury*, Harry Landers in *C-Man*. And the slowly fading romantic stars—Franchot Tone, George Brent, Robert Taylor—found that the colorful role of a psychotic killer, even if his true colors weren't revealed until the closing reel, was a pretty safe way of pepping up a faltering career. None of these stars could really be blamed if they chose obvious ways of expressing mental disorders; a sudden twitching, a staring of the eyes, a jerking of the head. At least they were a step forward from George Curzon, the psycho-killer in Alfred Hitchcock's excellent British thriller

The ambitious "B" film that started the psychiatry craze: *Blind Alley*. Ralph Bellamy is the doctor, Ann Dvorak the gangster's girl, and Chester Morris the nightmare-haunted killer. William Holden played the Morris role in a later remake, *The Dark Past*.

Joseph Cotten as the charming Uncle Charlie—actually a murderer of rich widows—in Hitchcock's *Shadow of a Doubt* (1943).

A well-done minor thriller of 1941: *Among the Living*, with Albert Dekker as the madman and Jean Phillips as the girl he kills.

of the mid-30's, *Young and Innocent*. Curzon went through the whole film with such a spectacular facial twitch that one wonders why he hadn't been locked up years before!

Thrillers with psychotics have never been terribly appetizing. There is a stigma, even if there shouldn't be, or if one refuses to admit it, to mental illness. One

Laird Cregar starred in the best of the Jack the Ripper films, *The Lodger* (1944).

A later Ripper: Jack Palance in *Man in the Attic* (1953), with Constance Smith.

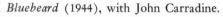
*Bluebeard* (1944), with John Carradine.

Charles Boyer as the wife-murderer, with Ingrid Bergman as his intended victim, in *Gaslight* (1944). In an earlier British version, Anton Walbrook played the role.

is usually uncomfortable about really enjoying and accepting a thriller built too realistically around mental imbalance. Thus in the past, producers have perhaps wisely cashed in on the superficial fascination of insanity, while sidestepping the physically repugnant details. Cast your mind back to the psycho thrillers of the past and you will see that most of them use neuroses rather facilely for *motivation*, but avoided blatant madness in *execution*. Franchot Tone in *Phantom Lady* and Basil Rathbone in *Love From a Stranger* were rather charming, and their scenes of menace were not markedly different from those afforded to "normal" villains. But in recent years, all this has changed. So many unpleasant and hitherto tabu subjects have found their way to the screen under the guise of "maturity" and "realism" that it was only to be expected that the psycho would get his share of screen time too. And he has: both in terms of sympathetic (but often embarassingly detailed) clinical study, as in such films as *Captain Newman, M.D.*, and more notably in terms of the sexually motivated psychotic killer. Two of the most dynamic of such villain

portrayals came from that under-rated and often wasted actor, Robert Mitchum. In *Night of the Hunter*, a pretentious but sincerely felt and artistically conceived thriller, the first and only film directed by Charles Laughton, Mitchum played a kind of modern Jack the Ripper. Partly motivated by greed, largely by a misdirected religious fervor, he kills women for the small monetary profit and the larger neurotic satisfaction of erasing what is to him a disgusting sexual object. Changing from warm charm to ice-cold venom within moments, screaming in frustration and pain, like some animal, when thwarted—or hurt—Mitchum created a truly remarkable portrait in that 1955 film. Then, seven years later, he created an equally striking villain in *Cape Fear*. Frankly a "sick" movie, with none of the artistic merit of its predecessor, though possessing an undeniable surface thrill and tension, it presented Mitchum as a vengeful ex-convict, out to even the score with the man who sent him to jail by hitting at him through his family. Conducting a slow and carefully legal campaign of terror, Mitchum makes it plain that he plans to rape the man's teen-age

193

*The Sea Wolf* (1941) rather re-shaped Jack London's adventure tale to stress the psychotic motivation of Edward G. Robinson's savagery; with Alexander Knox.

The original version of *Night Must Fall* (1937) with Dame May Whitty, Rosalind Russell, Robert Montgomery.

Lee Marvin, an excellent psycho villain of the fifties.

The 1964 remake of *Night Must Fall* with Albert Finney offered sledgehammer statements instead of subtle suggestion, and a liberal dosing of sex.

Hitchcock's *Strangers on a Train* (1951) starred Robert Walker as an obviously homosexual psycho.

Robert Mitchum in *Night of the Hunter*.

daughter and his wife—and he all but succeeds. The overall motivation was weak, however, and one had the uncomfortable feeling of a psychotic being exploited for fast-buck purposes.

If there is a "definitive" psycho film, it is prob- ably Alfred Hitchcock's equally sick—though more stylishly so—film appropriately titled *Psycho* (1960). In it, Tony Perkins was most effectively cast as an effeminate youth who adopts the manners, dress, voice and personality of his dead mother, and in moments

Mitchum and Polly Bergen in *Cape Fear* (1962).

Tony Perkins in *Psycho* (1960).

of stress becomes a knife-slashing killer. Hitchcock's film could well have been the last word on the subject, but it was far too successful at the boxoffice for that. Since then, several psychotic killers, going one up on Hitchcock by doing their dirty work with an axe instead of a knife, have become permanent additions to the stable of Hollywood badmen. Cashing in on *two* enormously successful films, one called itself *Anatomy of a Psycho*, while another, *Psychomania*, enticingly explained in its advertising that its villain was a sex-o-maniac!

One of the newer screen psychos, Victor Bueno slobbered his way to fame in *What Ever Happened to Baby Jane?*, was rewarded with the starring role in *The Strangler* (1964).

# MAD DOCTORS
## AND
### MAD KILLERS

The mad scientist inevitably overlaps into the territory of the monster, and since the monster—man-made or otherwise—got but scant attention in the pre-talkie years, it follows that the mad scientist was similarly overlooked. Dr. Jekyll and Mr. Hyde came to the screen several times, in increasingly long versions, finally hitting his (or their?) stride in 1920 when two versions were made competitively, and both in New York. The better of the duo was undoubtedly John Barrymore's, and the power and poignancy of his performance, and the skill with which the change overs from man to near-monster were accomplished, are remarkable still. Although Barrymore used bizarre make-up, the change overs themselves were done without camera tricks, and relied on the extraordinary way that he was able to distort and apparently elongate his features. The second adaptation of the Stevenson classic starred Sheldon Lewis, and was a much cheaper and cruder affair. To cut down on costs, the story was updated to contemporary New York, and it even had the temerity to tack on a happy ending by having the whole thing turn out to be a dream.

The traditional mad scientist turned up occasionally in the 1920's. *The Monster* (1925) was in the curious position of satirizing a genre that had not even been created yet! Lon Chaney played the rather tongue-in-cheek scientist who "arranged" road accidents near his mansion-laboratory, where he maintained a chamber of horrors. The whole film was a strange forerunner of the Karloff-Lugosi talkie *The Raven*. And, in 1926, a Somerset Maugham story, "The Magician," suggested by the career of notorious black-magic exponent Aleister Crowley, was brought

In *The Bells* (1925) Karloff played a mesmerist quite obviously "borrowed" from Dr. Caligari.

*The Black Cat* (1934) with Boris as the head of a devil-worshiping cult.

*The Black Cat* also found Bela Lugosi in a comparatively sympathetic role. He wound up skinning Karloff alive before blowing himself up.

*The Raven* (1935): Karloff sees for the first time the monstrous new face given him by surgeon Lugosi.

Lugosi, an Edgar Allan Poe fancier, finds himself trapped in his own "pit and pendulum" device and at Karloff's mercy; also from *The Raven*.

*The Invisible Ray* (1936) with Karloff and Frances Drake. Lugosi's co-starring role this time was a minor one.

to the screen with Alice Terry in the lead. Critics, blissfully unaware of the cycles of far grimmer horror films that were ahead, were unanimous in branding as "tasteless" the story of a scientist whose experiments call for the blood of a pure girl.

Sound brought *Frankenstein* to the screen, and with it a whole new world of crackling electrical machines and bubbling test-tubes. Since the doctor, mad or otherwise, could logically overlap into the worlds of monsters, vampires, voodoo, and later,

outer-space, he was to have a long and colorful career of movie crime ahead of him.

Depending on who played them, the scientists of the horror films were either sincere but misguided, with worthwhile if dangerous and impractical aims, or they were thoroughly insane and conducted experiments for the sake of glory, vanity, and self-gain.

All of the Frankensteins were thoroughly sane and reputable—but all of them, and they included Colin Clive, Basil Rathbone, and Sir Cedric Hardwicke,

In *The Black Room* (1935), Karloff was twin brothers—one good, one quite the reverse. This is the bad brother, attacking Katherine DeMille.

Boris returns from the grave once more in *The Walking Dead* (1936).

With the somewhat skeptical aid of daughter Amanda Duff, Karloff and his machines try to contact "the world beyond" in 1941's *The Devil Commands*.

202

were cursed with incredibly inefficient or selfishly motivated assistants, who were forever putting the wrong brain in the monster's skull, and guiding his instincts to murderous rather than peaceful ends. Boris Karloff's scientists, whether mad as a hatter or merely amiably bemused, were likewise completely sympathetic. Karloff's scientific notions were at least designed for the good of mankind, and included such interesting ideas as the restoration of life after death, the preservation of life through the use of artificial hearts, and the creation of suspended animation through freezing. Oddly enough, not a few of the ideas expounded in early horror films later proved to be medically quite sound.

Bela Lugosi, on the other hand, emulating Count Dracula, turned his scientific skill to diabolic and self-

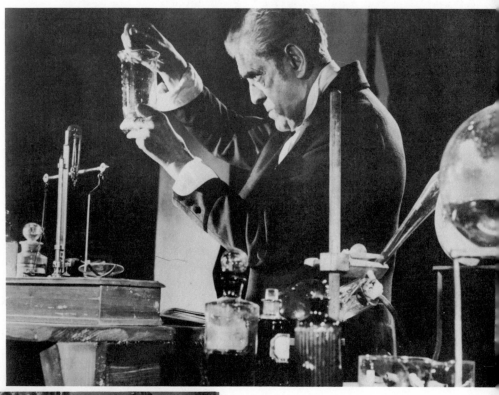

One of the more serious horror films of the sixties: Karloff as a pioneer in anesthesia in *Corridors of Blood* (1962).

Four grand old stalwarts: Karloff, Rathbone, Lorre and Price co-starred in another macabre spoof, *Comedy of Terrors* (1964).

203

Surgeon Lugosi admires his handi-
work on patient Karloff in *The
Raven* (1935).

As Dr. Orloff in the Edgar Wallace
thriller, *Dark Eyes of London*
(1939), Lugosi disposes of an
awkward witness.

Fellow scientist John Carradine is
sacrificed to the cause of medical
research by Lugosi, in *The Return
of the Ape Man*.

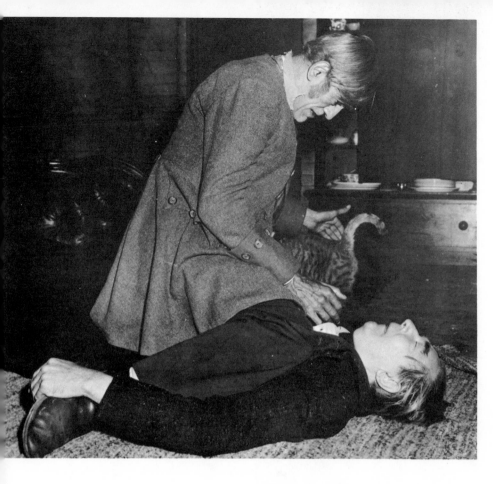

Lugosi once more dispatched by Karloff, in one of the most literate of horror films, *The Body Snatchers* (1945).

Lionel Atwill

satisfying ends. He kidnapped young brides in order to create a serum from their spinal fluids with which to keep alive his decaying crone of a wife. He perfected a shaving soap the scent of which drew his artificially enlarged killer bats to the throats of his enemies. And, at his most fiendish, in 1935's *The Raven*, he turned his medical and mechanical skill to the establishment of an Edgar Allan Poe torture chamber. Co-star Boris Karloff, a killer on the loose, comes to Lugosi for asylum— and a spot of plastic surgery. First of all, Lugosi taunts him with the knowledge of the recent murder Karloff has committed. Poor Karloff is embarassed, like a schoolboy caught playing truant. "Well, after all, he was in my way, and there was the acetelene torch in my hand," he begins lamely. Lugosi reminds him that he then thrust the blazing torch into the man's eyes. "Well, there are some things you can't 'elp doing," Karloff grumbles petulantly. Lugosi does agree to the operation, and Karloff emerges with his face considerably changed. One side of his face is horribly scarred, his lips are twisted, and one eye is several inches lower than the other. However, this is merely the beginning of Lugosi's monstrous behavior in a film far better seen than described. With stunning sets and marvellously full-blooded dialogue, *The Raven* gives Karloff and Lugosi their heads, and their delightful collaboration results in a film that is both a sharply-etched lampoon (if one chooses to take it that way) and an excellent Grand Guignol to boot.

Atwill, as the mad and deformed sculptor, tries to add Fay Wray to his exhibits in *The Mystery of the Wax Museum* (1933).

One of the most dignified and diabolical of the mad scientists was Lionel Atwill, who started out, like Karloff, as innately sympathetic villains. As the artist who is crazed when his life's work (a wax museum) is deliberately destroyed for fire insurance, and who turns to re-creating his models by putting corpses through a wax-coating process, he starred in one of the classic spine-chillers of the early 1930's, *The Mystery of the Wax Museum*. Its magnificent and eerie sets enhanced by the then-prevalent two-color Technicolor, it reached a stunning and shattering climax as

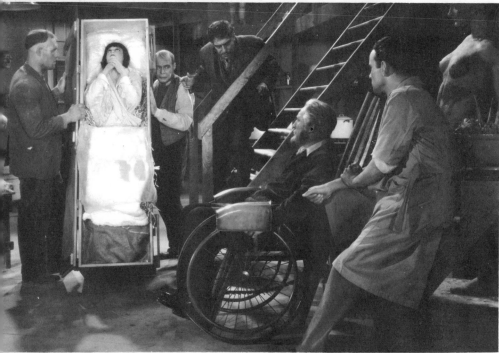

Another scene from the classic *Mystery of the Wax Museum*. Mathew Betz and Arthur Edmund Carewe are to the right of the casket.

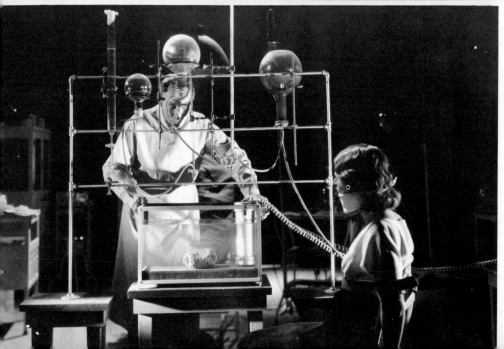

Later in 1933, Fay Wray was again offered "eternal life" by Atwill—in *The Vampire Bat*.

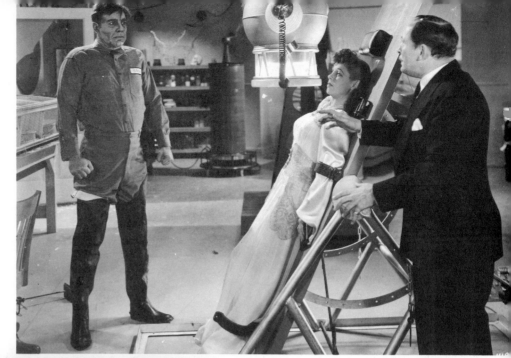

In 1941, business as usual. Anne Nagel is about to receive the gift of "eternal life" while Lon Chaney Jr., having already experienced it, is about to intervene, in *Man Made Monster*.

Rudolph Klein-Rogge as Rotwang, creator of a super-robot, in 1926's *Metropolis*.

the madman is about to put his live captive—Fay Wray—through the wax-coating process. The lovely Miss Wray, who screamed her way through three encounters with Lionel Atwill, and one apiece with Leslie Banks and King Kong, beats desperately at his face—which suddenly cracks and begins to fall apart.

A fine study of Ernest Thesiger, as he appeared with Lillian Bond, in *The Old Dark House* (1932).

207

As she claws further at his face, it disintegrates completely. Revealed beneath, looking like a gnarled walnut, are the hideous features of a man whose face has been completely burned away by that earlier wax-museum fire—and who has lived ever since behind a wax replica of his original face! It was one of the finest shock sequences in horror film history, equalled only by the unmasking scene in Lon Chaney's *Phantom of the Opera*. Ironically, this great horror classic, *The Mystery of the Wax Museum*—containing Atwill's finest performance—has itself now decayed into nothing. No prints or negatives are known to remain, but the remake—that early 3D film *The House of Wax*—does give a few hints as to the greatness of the original.

Atwill played another rather bizarre scientist in *Dr. X*, although in this instance he turned out *not* to be the murderer. Still, the film's best line of dialogue was his. Showing investigating detectives through his research clinic, he identifies his staff, all of whom get a kind of half-apologetic introduction, since one is deformed, another has long been suspected of cannibalism, and a third seems strangely affected by the moon. Finally, one of the doctors so introduced complains that his arm is painful—and, casually unscrewing it, places the artificial limb on a table in front of him. Never wavering, and with superb aplomb, Atwill turns to the detectives. "Come, gentlemen," he says cheerfully, "there are many more interesting things to see!"

Ernest Thesiger displays some of his creations in *The Bride of Frankenstein*.

Thesiger as Dr. Praetorius, a marvelously flamboyant, mad scientist in *The Bride of Frankenstein*. (1935).

John Barrymore in *Dr. Jekyll and Mr. Hyde* (1920), first really important adaptation of the Stevenson novel.

Lucien Littlefield (with Gertrude Astor and Laura LaPlante) was another Caligari-inspired doctor in *The Cat and the Canary* (1927).

Lionel Atwill's scientific career did not maintain the integrity of Karloff's. Soon he was off on harebrained schemes to raise armies of electrical supermen with which he would rule the world. All such scientists had two basic lines of dialogue, and Atwill delivered them on more than one occasion. The first was when the heroine rather tactlessly accused him of being mad, and Atwill would reply with a "Mad? Of course I'm mad!"—and launch into a tirade wherein he listed all of the other great scientists—from Galileo to Pasteur—who had been thought mad because they were ahead of their time! And the second block-busting line would be when he'd grab the heroine in the climactic reel, and, just before strapping her to his apparatus, would cheer her up with "Think of it, my dear! I offer you eternal life!"

Atwill, Karloff, and Lugosi seemed to have a rival for a while in Ernest Thesiger, the hawk-nosed British actor who played the insane Dr. Praetorius in *The Bride of Frankenstein*. With his Satanic expression and rich dialogue-delivery, Thesiger brought a mordant sense of humor to his scientist that was quite refreshing. But while he played strong character roles in one or two other horror films, he played the mad scientist once only—as did two other British character actors, Claude Rains (in *The Invisible Man*) and Charles Laughton (*Island of Lost Souls*).

Of the challengers to the supremacy of Atwill,

Fredric March in the 1932 version, the grimmest of several adaptations.

Karloff, and Lugosi, George Zucco came the closest. Another British actor (as, for that matter, were Karloff and Atwill), he played his mad scientists with a supercilious condescension, and had a way of making his eyes light up like neons whenever he thought of anything particularly revolting. But, by the time Zucco was ensconced in horror films, the genre had sunk to standardized programmer level, and he was never able to devise anything more original than trans-planting a man's brain into the head of a gorilla—always a rather pointless procedure—and developing a poison gas that created a death-like trance and required a fresh human heart to restore life, another medical venture of somewhat dubious practical value. Otto Kruger, John Carradine, J. Carrol Naish, and Leo G. Carroll were others who joined in equally suspect medical ventures in the 1940's and 1950's.

None of the horror specialists here discussed

Spencer Tracy's 1940 "Jekyll and Hyde" was less gruesome, more Freudian.

Mad scientist Charles Laughton and ape-man creation in *Island of Lost Souls* (1932).

limited themselves solely to the mad doctor of course, though the role did seem to occupy the bulk of their time. Boris Karloff, the finest actor them all, understandably achieved the greatest variety; his colorful malefactors include several bizarre brands of murderers, a man brought back to life from the dead, a sinister head of a Devil-worshipping cult, a grave-robber (one of his finest performances, in that literate and exciting film *The Body Snatchers*), a deaf-mute giant of a butler, and the corrupt governor of an

Claude Rains outlines his insane plan for world domination to frightened fiancée Gloria Stuart in *The Invisible Man* (1933).

Peter Lorre as the scientist who grafts a murderer's hands onto the arms of a pianist in *Mad Love* (1935), a remake of the German classic, *Hands of Orlac*; with Frances Drake.

Albert Dekker used radium rays to reduce humans to doll size in *Dr. Cyclops* (1940).

212

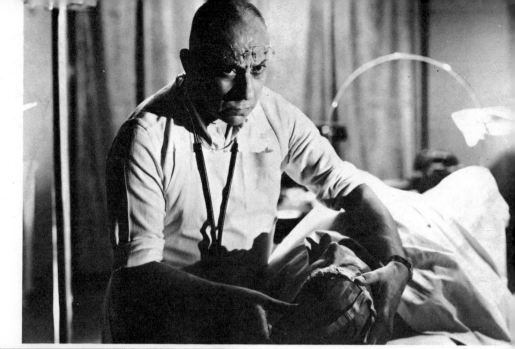

Erich von Stroheim in *The Lady and the Monster* (1944), first of three adaptations of Curt Siodmak's "Donovan's Brain."

George Zucco, who was infinitely superior to the grade-C mad scientist affairs (*The Mad Ghoul, The Flying Serpent*) in which he so frequently found himself.

Scientist Alan Napier and creature "Atlas" (Glenn Strange, who also played the Frankenstein monster on three occasions) in *Master Minds* (1949).

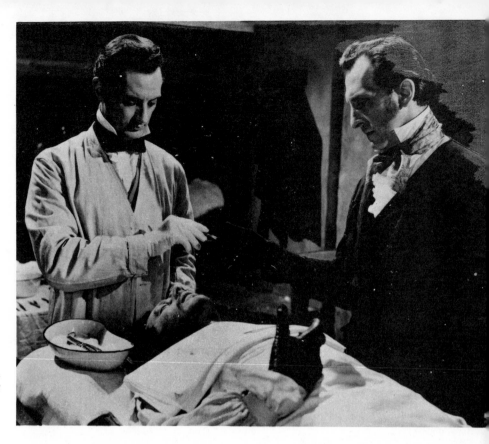

Peter Cushing (right), the new Dr. Frankenstein; from 1958's *Revenge of Frankenstein*.

Lon Chaney Jr., in *The Haunted Palace* (1963).

asylum. But, in the late 1950's and early 1960's, he began to devote himself to science again—as a distant relative of the original scientist in *Frankenstein 1970*, and as the discoverer of anathesia in (presumably and hopefully!) larger-than-life retelling of that momentous event, titled *Corridors of Blood*. In such films, and in such films only, is the mad doctor and dedicated scientist still with us. Science itself has now outgrown the scientist, and in this post-atomic age, with the world forever threatened by outer-space phenomena, the scientist's role is to combat the evil from without—*not* to contribute to it.

# THE
# BAD
# GIRLS

Theda Bara in action again, in 1919.

Even though this book is dedicated to the bad *guys*, it would be both ungentlemanly—and historically unfair—to by-pass the ladies completely. Since their villainy covered the same ground as their male counterparts, it is obviously impossible to do them justice in this one postscript, but they at least rate an approving nod in passing. For there have been lady gangsters, lady cattle-rustlers, lady mad doctors, lady vampires, lady spies, lady monsters, lady brutes, and lady psychos. Even some of those incredibly hooded mystery villains in serials and melodramas turned out to be ladies—and in some fields the weaker sex quite outshone the males! No one will dispute that the vamps made a far greater impression on audiences and box offices than the gigolos. And no male was ever able to match the deceit, cunning, and sheer cold-blooded ruthlessness of the kind of queen-bee female so expertly played by Bette Davis in *Of Human Bondage*, *The Little Foxes*, and *In This Our Life*. For the bad girl was able to use her sex in an *oppressive* as well as an aggressive and provocative way. What mere male (overlooking the biological limitations for a moment) would even think of getting his way by using the feminine arsenal of tears, feigned (or actual) pregnancy, and that always reliable old standby, the "splitting headache"?

The bad girls really came into their own in the movies in 1914, when the vamp was created to do all the colorful and interesting things that the good girls (Mary Pickford, Lillian Gish) were forbidden to do.

Louise Glaum, Theda's principal rival, tried to vamp William S. Hart in several early westerns.

216

Nita Naldi, as Dona Sol, uses her wiles on Rudolph Valentino in *Blood and Sand* (1922).

The 1941 remake of *Blood and Sand* saw Rita Hayworth vamping Tyrone Power.

Mae Busch joins in a little degenerate horseplay with Erich von Stroheim in *Foolish Wives* (1922).

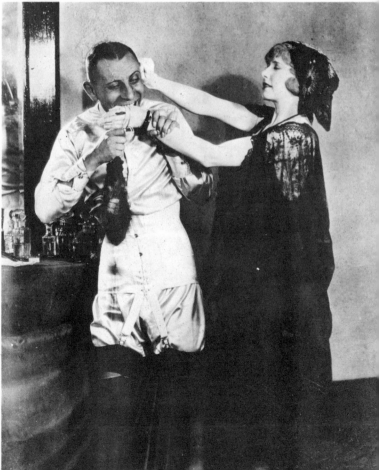

In the thirties Mae turned in some fine cameos as a shrewish wife, a scheming blackmailer, and a prostitute with*out* a heart of gold in several Laurel and Hardy comedies. This one: *Come Clean* (1931).

Helen Gardner and the very beautiful Viola Barry had essayed femme fatales as early as 1912, but it wasn't until 1914's *A Fool There Was* that the vamp was really launched—and, with her, one of the biggest box office draws of those early days, Theda Bara. In those days, merely drinking and smoking in public was enough to brand a woman as an unredeemable sinner, but tobacco and liquor were just props with which Theda set the stage. Enticingly gowned in macabre costumes decorated with spider webs and bat wings,

*Variety*: Lya de Putti with Emil Jannings.

Lya de Putti, the "tramp" bad girl in the German classic *Variety* (1926).

One of the most devastating of all movie man-killers: Margaret Livingston with George O'Brien in her power in 1927's *Sunrise*.

the better to suggest the predatory beast of prey seeking out a victim, heavily mascaraed, and with a sullen smile that betrayed her utter contempt for her male victims, Theda was a literal man-killer. More than one of her victims, disgraced, degraded, financially ruined, took suicide as the only way out. Nobody took Theda too seriously—her movies were old-fashioned *then*, and while it would be exaggerating to say that they were done tongue-in-cheek, audiences never really believed in Theda's sinning quite as much as they did in Mary's purity. Her films were warnings of hellfire and brimstone—with showmanship. Moviegoers were able to watch some lavish helpings of forbidden fruit for an hour or so, and talk themselves into believing that they had learned a moral lesson!

Theda and her rival vampires, Louise Glaum and Valeska Suratt, held sway until about 1920, when their power was broken by the "good girl" star finding that she could display a little sex too and *not* lose her public support. For a while, the vamps hit back. In the delectable forms of Nita Naldi, Carmel Myers, and others, they became sleeker, smoother, less obvious (though no less aggressive) and far sexier. Nita Naldi's sensuous seduction of Rudolph Valentino in *Blood and Sand* is

Joan Bennett with an enslaved Edward G. Robinson in *Scarlet Street* (1945).

Rita Hayworth and Orson Welles in *The Lady from Shanghai* (1948).

Lana Turner as the sexy trollop who persuades her boy friend (John Garfield) to murder her husband in *The Postman Always Rings Twice* (1946).

still something of a landmark in such steamy scenes. But there was a difference; the old vamps wrecked their men's lives completely, and usually emerged triumphant. The new vamps could divert them for a while—but ultimately their victims would return to their wives and sweethearts, some of whom learned a lesson from the vamps and themselves adopted more physically alluring methods. As soon as the heroine

In the forties, Barbara Stanwyck built a whole new career around temptresses and murderesses; with Van Heflin in *The Strange Love of Martha Ivers* (1946).

Mary Astor as the double-dealing murderess-"heroine" of *The Maltese Falcon* (1941), with Bogart.

could do all that the vamp could do—and get away with it—the vamp all but disappeared. If she remained, it was usually as the sophisticated "other woman" in sex comedies, or, occasionally, in remakes of earlier hits —as when Rita Hayworth re-did the Nita Naldi role in the sound version of *Blood and Sand*.

With the disappearance of the vamp genre at the end of the 1920's, woman's dominance in one specific branch of villainy came to an end. But her crimes in what were more specifically male preserves continued unchecked. The female vampires in *Dracula* had less to do than Bela Lugosi—but in their silent glidings about the deserted castle, and in their patient watching and waiting, they were perhaps even more menacing. Westerns (*The Old Chisholm Trail* is a good example) occasionally used female villains too. They had a special advantage in the Old West, and they knew it. They could rustle the hero's cattle and he, as a kind of composite Knight and Boy Scout, could do little about it. (Fortunately, he usually had an athletic leading lady who *could* take on the villainess in a climactic fist-fight!)

After the gangster classic *Scarface*, it was inevitable that a few years later there would be a "Lady Scarface." And, in *Queen of the Mob*, Blanche Yurka made every bit as ruthless a gang leader as Robinson or Cagney had done.

Serials, enjoying a new lease on life in the 1940's, went back to the silent chapter-plays for much of their inspiration, and came up with not just new serial queens, but new serial villainesses too. Lorna Gray, as Vultura, assisted by a pet gorilla called Satan, made life very difficult for Kay Alridge in *The Perils of Nyoka*, and spent a good percentage of the serial

Linden Travers, one of the best "bad girls" of British movies, with Jack LaRue in *No Orchids for Miss Blandish* (1950).

devising picturesque and complicated tortures to which the attractive heroine, fetchingly clad in tight blouse and skirt, could be subjected. Over at Columbia, Carol Forman was the Spider Woman in a Superman serial, while Universal had their own Spider Woman in the form of Gale Sondergaard. In the horror film, *The Spider Woman Strikes Back* (she had done her initial striking in a Sherlock Holmes adventure a year or so earlier) Miss Sondergaard had worked out an incredibly complicated scheme of personal revenge on local ranchers whom she felt were occupying land rightfully hers. Advertising for companions, she then drugged them, siphoned off their blood, fed it to giant carnivorous plants that she cultivated, and from the plants brewed a mysterious poison that killed off the ranchers' cattle and brought them to bankruptcy. Fred Kohler or Charles King, with a few hand-picked rustlers, could have achieved the same end with *far* less trouble!

Concurrently in the 1940's, the revival of interest in the high-class detective and mystery thrillers based on stories by authors such as Dashiell Hammett and Raymond Chandler, brought some unusually interesting villainesses to the screen. Mary Astor as the seemingly angelic "heroine" of *The Maltese Falcon*—actually a double-crossing murderess—was quite superb, and far surpassed even Bebe Daniels and Bette

Kathleen Byron, a specialist in bitchy and neurotic villainesses, and remembered as the nymphomaniac nun who goes berserk in *Black Narcissus*, here seen with Guy Rolfe in *The Reluctant Widow* (1950).

Bette Davis in *The Letter* (1940).

Bette Davis in one of the best of her many "bad girl" roles, with Charles Coburn in *In This Our Life* (1942).

Less subtle but equally vicious Davis villainy in *What Ever Happened to Baby Jane?* (1962).

Beautiful Louise Brooks, a sympathetic and misunderstood "bad girl," in the 1929 *Diary of a Lost Girl* with her seducer, Fritz Rasp. .

Davis, who had played the same role in earlier versions. (The second version, *Satan Met a Lady*, had been reshaped slightly so that it also had a *second* feminine villain—the large Alison Skipworth, in the Sydney Greenstreet role). Claire Trevor in *Murder, My Sweet* was another of the tough babes whose crimes included murder in this colorful and exciting period.

In the late 1940's and 1950's, there was a certain tendency for the bad girl to be basically sympathetic, for her crimes to be forced on her by circumstance and emotional upsets rather than through calculation. Jennifer Jones in *Duel in the Sun* and *Ruby Gentry*, and Peggy Cummings in *Gun Crazy*, are typical examples. But the increasing popularity of taut crime melodramas brought us a prodigious array of criminal bitchery, with lovely, warm, sophisticated ladies casually arranging wholesale double-crosses, or arranging with their paramours to murder their husbands for the insurance. Remember Bette Davis in *Another Man's Poison*, Barbara Stanwyck in *Double Indemnity* and *The Strange Love of Martha Ivers*, Ann Savage in

Anna May Wong, Oriental villainess of *The Thief of Bagdad, In Old San Francisco* and many other silent and talkie melodramas.

Two of the most despicable villainesses of the late thirties were witches—in *Snow White and the Seven Dwarfs* (1937) and *The Wizard of Oz* (1939), as played by Margaret Hamilton.

Olga Baclanova as the "Feathered Hen," a former trapeze beauty mutilated by circus freaks; from *Freaks* (1931).

Dracula's vampire wives in *Dracula* (1931).

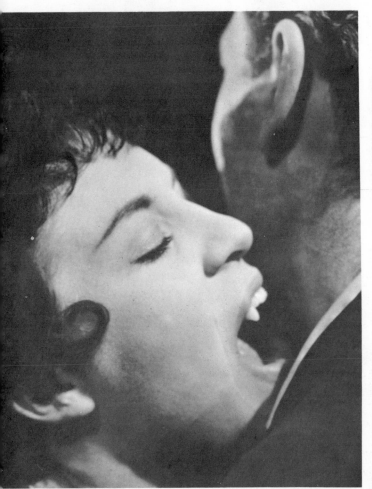

Another female vampire following in the Lugosi tradition in *Horror of Dracula* (1958).

Annette Vadim as a decidedly sensuous vampire in *Blood and Roses* (1960).

Marla English as the "She-Creature," one of several off-beat (and mildly erotic) horror-thrillers made by producer Alex Gordon in the mid-1950's.

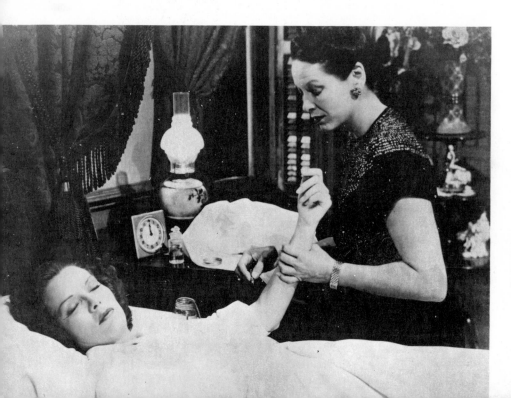

Gale Sondergaard (right) prepares to steal some blood from the drugged Brenda Joyce in *The Spider Woman Strikes Back* (1946).

"Bad girl" Vultura (Lorna Gray) temporarily has the upper hand in a struggle with "good girl" Nyoka (Kay Aldridge) in the 1941 serial *The Perils of Nyoka*.

Viviane Romance, one of France's most delectable vamps, in and as *Carmen* (1947).

Harriet Anderson made an intriguing Swedish "bad girl," since many of her indiscretions were committed in the nude. From Ingmar Bergman's *The Naked Night* (1955).

A bad girl almost all the time . . . but a villainess almost never: Brigitte Bardot in *And God Created Woman* (1956).

*Decoy*, Linda Darnell in *Fallen Angel*, Lizabeth Scott in *Dead Reckoning*, Lana Turner in *The Postman Always Rings Twice*, Ann Blyth in *Mildred Pierce*, and Ava Gardner in *The Killers*? Indeed, in retrospect, the 1940's seem to have spawned more notable female villains than any period in film history—in part perhaps because with so many top male stars in the armed forces during those war years, the women rather took over the Hollywood scene. If there were more vicious crime films in the 1940's than there had been for quite a while, there were also more emotional stories and love stories in the old tradition too. The exag-

Marlene Dietrich: tramp, B-girl, hustler, thief, destroyer of men and toppler of thrones—the most devastating "bad girl" of them all.

Anne Baxter, the outwardly sweet and straightforward girl who can inwardly be the psycho of *Guest in the House*, the murderess of *The Come On* or, most famous of all, the schemer of *All About Eve* (1950).

Claire Trevor and Dick Powell in *Murder, My Sweet* (1944).

"Bad girl" Diana Dors and "good girl" Odile Versois in *Room 43*. Their state of dress should surely be sufficient identification as to which is which!

Since Shelley Winters has played the madam of a bordello at least twice in the past two years (this scene is from 1963's *The Balcony*), she surely qualifies as a "bad girl" *now*—but ten years hence, who knows?

gerated virtue of Greer Garson in *Random Harvest* and *Blossoms in the Dust* helped balance the equally exaggerated viciousness of Stanwyck and Gardner.

With the men back from the wars and in command again, the ladies settled down to more normal pursuits. But they appeared to be merely biding their time. Every so often a performance like Anne Baxter's in *All About Eve*, Marilyn Monroe's in *Niagara*, or Kim Novak's in *Pushover*, would remind us of the marvellous volcanic power the ladies could muster when they had a villain role they could get their teeth into. And something else was happening, too. Holly-

wood's star system was faltering. The big male names were disappearing. Power, Flynn, Bogart, Colman, Cooper, and Gable died; Cary Grant. though as virile and good-looking as ever, was reaching his sixties. With a start, one realized that even such comparatively "new" stars as Gregory Peck, Glenn Ford, and William Holden had been in movies for a quarter of a century or more. And the newer stars who were coming along just didn't have that extra something that Gable and Cooper and Bogart had when they were young and starting out.

It began to look as though the women were taking

Peggie Castle, an expert at playing silken mistresses and gangland come-ons, in *I, the Jury* (1953).

Barbara Payton with Lloyd Bridges in *Trapped* (1949).

To be up to date, the current "bad girl" must mix a little perversion, sadism or neurotic imbalance in with her wrongdoing. Example: Anita Ekberg in *The Mongols* (1962).

over again, and not least in villainous fields. Martha Hyer, although yet to be properly exploited, has proven (*Desire in the Dust*, etc.) to be one of the most thoroughly exciting—and despicable—movie bitches since Stanwyck and Turner at their peak. Elizabeth Taylor is far more exciting as a bad girl (*Butterfield 8*) than as a good girl (*Raintree County*). And now, in early 1964, the dam is beginning to burst. After last year's successful *What Ever Happened to Baby Jane?* the old pros—as well as the new young hopefuls—are turning to crime and horror. In the first two months of 1964, we had Bette Davis in a dual role as sisters, both of them murderers; Lauren Bacall as a madwoman; and Joan Crawford as an axe-killer. Kim Novak is on the horizon with Somerset Maugham's classic slut, Mildred, in *Of Human Bondage*. And there are more to come. The 1960's may well wind up outdoing even the 1940's in becoming *the* period that future film historians will regard as the golden age of the bad girls.

Joan Crawford is an axe-murderess in *Straitjacket* (1963)—and in a sense she is the heroine too. Rather a far cry from those happy, innocent days when merely smoking or drinking (let alone both!) promptly stamped any screen character as a woman of sin!

# GENERAL INDEX

233

# PICTURE INDEX